The Power of Buddhism

Tenzin Gyatso, His Holiness the Dalai Lama, is the spiritual leader of Tibetan Buddhists. Since the invasion of Tibet by China in 1959, he has been living in exile in Dharamsala, India. In 1989, he was awarded the Nobel Peace Prize for his efforts towards the liberation of Tibet through peaceful resolutions.

Jean-Claude Carrière is a French writer, actor and 2014 Academy Award honoree. In 2015, he was awarded the Padma Shri for his work in the field of literature and education. Other than novels, he has also written the screenplay for more than forty films, including *The Return of Martin Guerre*, *The Unbearable Lightness of Being* and *The Mahabharata*. He lives in France.

The Power of Buddhism

THE DALAI LAMA

AND

JEAN-CLAUDE CARRIÈRE

MOTILAL BANARSIDASS
SINCE 1903 IN INDOLOGY

Originally published in French in France as *La force du bouddhisme* by Éditions Robert Laffont.

First published in English in the United States as *Violence and Compassion* in 1996 by Image Books.

This edition published by arrangement with Image Books, an imprint of Crown Publishing Group, a division of Penguin Random House LLC.

This edition first published in India 2017 by Pan
an imprint of Pan Macmillan Publishing India Private Limited
707, Kailash Building
26, K. G. Marg, New Delhi – 110 001
www.panmacmillan.co.in

Pan Macmillan, 20 New Wharf Road, London N1 9RR
Basingstoke and Oxford
Associated companies throughout the world
www.panmacmillan.com

ISBN 978-81-208-4212-0

3 5 7 9 8 6 4 2

Typeset by Manmohan Kumar
Printed and bound in India by
Replika Press Pvt. Ltd.

Contents

Background

These conversations took place at McLeod Ganj, near Dharamsala, in northern India, in the month of February 1993 – more precisely, in the audience room of the Dalai Lama. Having arrived on February 10, I was able to attend the festival of the Tibetan New Year, which begins on February 11 at around five o'clock in the morning. I stayed at McLeod Ganj for two weeks.

I have to thank Laurent Laffont for giving me the idea for this book, as well as for organizing the trip. I have met the Dalai Lama briefly on two previous occasions, in the course of his two most recent journeys to France. I first contacted the officials in charge of the Bureau du Tibet in Paris, and thanks to them everything went off smoothly. When I recall that trip, apart from the preparatory work, which I obviously had to do and which took months, I'll always keep the memory of those deeply satisfying days. In particular the atmosphere of the monastery struck me as at once serious and smiling, with no hurry and no tension.

Before the trip, upon request from the Dalai Lama, I wrote a number of letters spelling out the topics that I wanted to touch on. These dealt, as might be imagined, with the possible role of

Buddhism in today's world and with its increasingly powerful appeal. We wished to discuss Buddhism in relation to our everyday life, to politics, to other religions or traditions, laying special emphasis on violence, the environment, and education. I quickly realized – and Buddhism teaches this anyway – that no one part can be separated from everything else, that every one of our words was caught up in a net of relations stretching out to infinity. It was impossible to isolate this or that subject from the whole body of the Buddhist attitude. In fact, I had to talk about everything, while avoiding the complex details of Buddhist teaching, mythology, and ritual.

I knew that the Dalai Lama was as much in demand as anyone in the world. So since we were short of time (and would a lifetime have been enough anyhow?), I suggested *not* questioning him on the points of doctrine or practice that he has already worked out in several of his books, instead, when the occasion prompted, I would borrow here and there from those works. He immediately accepted this proposal, which saved us a lot of time.

It quickly became apparent that the principal problem would be the level of readership. To whom should we address ourselves? Since neither of us wanted to limit our audience to specialists (I'm no specialist myself anyhow) and open this book to the greatest number, stoppages in the dialogue very soon seemed indispensable.

One might say that the Dalai Lama was admirably familiar with the ideas he discussed, that I have some notion of them, and that the majority of our readers risked either not knowing them or of understanding them superficially – that is to say, falsely.

Thus I made the decision, in agreement with the Dalai Lama, to interrupt our conversations every time I thought it necessary to explain this or that point. Needless to say, the whole volume has been checked by the Dalai Lama and his co-workers.

On this matter, I have to thank the officials of the Bureau du Tibet in Paris, Dawa Thondup and Wangpo Bashi. At McLeod Ganj, besides the conversations with His Holiness the Dalai Lama, I was able to refine certain points with his assistance and interpreter, Lhakdor, as well as with Kelsang Gyaltsen, both of whom were very pleasant and competent. I also want to thank Nahal Tajadod, a sinologist and specialist in the religions of central Asia. Her help and presence were valuable to me.

Our conversations took place in the audience room of Thekchen Choeling. Each of them lasted nearly three hours. We spoke English, but often enough the Dalai Lama abruptly switched to Tibetan, and then asked Lhakdor to translate for me what he had said. I recorded everything we said, and in the evening I deciphered and transcribed the day's dialogues.

I wrote this book in Paris in the months following my return. I stuck to the general order of our discussions, though at times I felt the necessity of regrouping some themes and better articulating the questions and answers. Since for all that this is a conversation, the reader will not be surprised to see certain phrases recurring. I felt I had to keep these repetitions so as not to rob the book of a certain vital disorder that follows a winding path, simple at first and gradually widening in all directions.

Neither of us wanted to publish a new catechism. On the contrary, we wanted to try to set up a real dialogue, constantly open and unexpected, drawing us into rarely travelled territory. I also made an effort to avoid both paralyzing respect and pointless disrespect. If I myself speak rather often and at some length, it's because my interlocutor wanted me to. He asked me questions and – something one meets with less frequently – he listened to me.

So this book has to be taken for what it is, a sort of walk, ordered and disordered, very attentive, with the best possible companion. It is not a study or a formal exposition. I repeat, many points of doctrine are barely touched on, and the extreme complexity of Mahayana Buddhism is merely alluded to. At issue here are some human phenomena that trouble us as much today as ever before, and sometimes more than before. And so I thought it essential to listen to a voice that speaks simply, by constantly relying on more than twenty centuries of reflection and experience.

Jean-Claude Carrière
Paris, France

1

This World Where We Live

The one who asks the question is mistaken.
The one who answers it is mistaken.
– The Buddha

We are comfortably seated around a rather large, low table, in the bright room where every day he receives visitors from all over the world. Across from me there is an effigy of the Buddha Sakyamuni, surrounded by other images and by statuettes, some of which managed to be saved from Tibet during the Dalai Lama's dramatic departure in 1959. Among these statuettes is one of Padmasambhava, the great Kashmiri preacher who was the true apostle of Buddhism to Tibet, in the eighth century.

In the center of the room is a stove. Outside, through the windows one sees trees and the snowy summits of the Himalayas. One can often hear crows cawing. The Dalai Lama is always accompanied by two assistants, one of whom, Lhakdor, serves as his interpreter when he slips from English into Tibetan.

At the beginning of each meeting, the Dalai Lama unties his shoelaces, takes off his shoes, and sits in the lotus position in his armchair. Like Lhakdor, he wears the simple red robe of the monks, the *bhiksus,* a garment that leaves the right arm bare.

After more than an hour of discussion, another smiling monk brings tea on a tray. Later the Dalai Lama puts his shoes back on, clearly signalling that the conversation is over. Everything is calm and warm, there is no perceptible tension. It seems true that echoes of the wars shaking the world can't reach this far. Sitting right next to me, the man whom everyone here calls His Holiness, Tenzin Gyatso, the fourteenth Dalai Lama, looks at me and listens calmly and attentively.

When people look at our world today, their feelings about the current state of humanity generally fall into one or two categories: one is fairly optimistic, but the other is much less so. These categories are well represented by two traditions of Eastern thought.

The first view is from Hindu tradition, in the idea of Kali Yuga, which is the dark era that began more than three thousand years ago, the day after the death of Krishna. This is an epoch of destruction where all hope is lost. It is the great darkness, the end of all virtue, the disappearance of the Dharma (the correct order) from the world. It is the triumph of ambition, of falsehood. There's no sense resisting: everything must disappear. A cycle ends in drought, famine, battles, with the bonds of society shattered. As the Mahabharata says, this is the time of lazy, cowardly, and cynical men. The earth – dead and hot – then falls prey to fire, and ends in a slow apocalypse. The sleep of Vishnu then envelopes the rediscovered nothingness, and the god dreams of the beauties of this world so that they won't be forgotten. Only after a very long time will Brahma the creator spring from Vishnu's navel and with a single stroke bring another world into existence.

The other more hopeful tradition affirms exactly the contrary. We are living – without knowing it – in an epoch of virtue, of mutual aid, of better observance of the Scriptures, a fortunate period.

Of these two traditions which one should we choose?

Without hesitation, the second. I say this for at least three reasons. First of all, it seems to me that the concept of war has recently changed. In the twentieth century, up until the years from 1960 to 1970, we still thought that the final and indisputable decision would come from a war. It was a matter of a very ancient law: the winners are right. Victory is the sign that God, or the gods, are on their side. Consequently, the victors impose their law on the vanquished, most often by means of a treaty, which will never be anything but a pretext for revenge. Hence the importance of arms and above all of nuclear arms, the central element of the Kali Yuga. The race for the bomb has imposed upon the earth a real danger of annihilation.

You think the danger is lessening?

Yes, I'm convinced it is. The Cold War seems to be over. The nuclear arsenals are being reduced. Who could complain of that?

And yet at this very moment there are more than fifty wars going on in the world: in Afghanistan, in Kashmir, in the battle between Muslims and Hindus on Indian territory. Not the least of which is the situation in the former Yugoslavia where 'ethnic cleansing' and nonstop artillery bombardment are destroying the country. Yet all of Europe hesitates about taking any action. No one would dare claim in good faith that we are less cruel than we used to be.

I know. These local wars are very cruel. And bad, of course. All wars, big or little, are negative. They reveal what is worst in us and only lead to new conflicts. But no place on the surface of the earth is safe from the nuclear threat. At least the little wars are limited. Here, today, at Dharamsala it seems to me that we are tranquil. It's true that many of these wars have broken out because of the removal of the nuclear threat.

Do you have other reasons for optimism?

Yes. Here's the second one: I believe that despite certain appearances the notion of *Ahimsa*, or nonviolence, is scoring some points. In the time of Mahatma Gandhi, a man whom I revere, nonviolence was mostly taken to be a weakness, a refusal to act, almost cowardice. This is no longer true. The choice of nonviolence is nowadays a positive act, which evokes a real force. Look at South Africa, and at what Arafat and Rabin have done. For several decades Palestinians and Israelis have seen, have proclaimed, have made use of nothing but force. The two sides have moved from there to peaceful negotiation.

Not without serious misgivings on both sides. And that leads to the reality of assassinations, of massacres, of teaching extermination to children on both sides.

To be sure. You don't have to tell me about the horrors of which we're capable. But the example given by the Palestinians and the Israeli government is still a good one, and it's been well received in the rest of the world.* And I have another feeling. I think that as a

* In March 1993, a few weeks after our discussions, the Dalai Lama visited Israel, where he met Jews, Muslims, Christians, Druzes, even Bahals. He visited Christian churches, the mosque of Omar, the Wailing Wall, and other places. He also spoke at length – but separately – with Palestinians and Israelis, on the need for peace. Though he thinks that the rift is still deep, he maintains that he got excellent 'vibrations' from both sides.

result of the press itself, of all the things we call communications, religious groups are visiting one another more often, and are getting to know one another better than they did before.

That's not true in some Muslim countries. On the contrary, they often have a tendency to close up within themselves in order to keep away all foreign influences, especially Western ones. In Algeria, groups of activists go as far as killing foreigners. That's an enterprise as absurd as it is bloody, and seems to go against the very spirit of the time. This then gives birth to more radically conflicting groups, which kill those who are supposed to be killing them, and so on. It gets worse and worse very quickly.

Isolation is never good for a country; and it's become impracticable. In the first half of the century Tibet had very few contacts with other peoples or with other traditions; and that did us a great deal of harm. Time left us behind, and we got a rude awakening. As for the Muslim countries, even if some of them maintain and reinforce their closed doors, on the whole, if one looks at the whole world, isolation is losing ground. For twenty years now I've been visiting many countries. Everywhere I go people tell me, 'We're getting to know one another better.'

Under the tolerant Tang dynasty from the seventh to the tenth century, there was a center for learning in northwest China, in the Turpan region. At this site, Taoists, Buddhists, Nestorian Christians, and Manichaeans (the latter two groups from Iran) met, exchanged texts, and went to great lengths to become better acquainted. The rule was to insist on common ground and to pass over differences.

No doubt we need such centres. And it would be an excellent idea to create some. For my part, I meet with other religious leaders as often as possible. We walk together, we visit one religious site or another, whatever tradition it may belong to. And there we meditate together, we share a moment of silence. I get a great sense of well-being from that. I continue to believe that in the domain of religion we are making progress by comparison with the beginning of the century.

Many commentators say the opposite. Everywhere one hears talk, even among Christians and Hindus, of the rise of fundamentalist movements.

That rise is real and disturbing. Some people see in it a reaction to the old terrors of the end of the millennium.

Or some secret compensation for the breakdown of ideologies. Others wonder why the ecumenical hopes of the 1950s seem to have given way to a growing fragmentation of beliefs. Sects are proliferating everywhere, differences get exacerbated. In Waco, Texas, David Koresh preferred to die in flames with his followers rather than surrender to the police.

From my own experience, I recently attended a series of lectures in Bombay dealing with the history of Zoroastrianism. Once the religion of Iran, this religion today has only about 80,000 followers who live mostly in Maharashtra, India. One of the lectures was about the influences Zoroastrianism underwent after the invasion of Iran by the Arabs in the seventh century. One of these influences came from Manichaeism, another religion that had already been exiled. In order to adapt to new territories deeply penetrated by Buddhism, the two traditions were obliged to adopt a vocabulary and certain ideas from Buddhism.

That's often the case.

Well, this was a purely linguistic study, based on inscriptions from that time. At the end of the lecture a rather portly individual (he looked like a businessman) got up and loudly proclaimed that Zoroastrianism could never have gotten deformed nor undergone any outside influence. He insisted Ahura Mazda was the one true God and Zoroaster was his only prophet. These declarations were accompanied by several political and racial remarks, such as, 'We are the only true Aryans.' I was stunned. I had just discovered, in this day and age, a Zoroastrian fundamentalist. I didn't know what answer to give him.

What percentage of the Parsees did he represent?

From what I was told, about 8 percent.

Well, 92 percent is the answer!* The human race is like that. It's always been like that. Don't touch that angry man. Leave him in peace. And if the majority of the Parsees refuse to follow him, let's just say: so much the better.

Is Buddhism safe from fundamentalism?

The very principles of Buddhism are the opposite of fundamentalism. On the contrary, they say that we are swept by a mighty stream, that nothing is stable forever.

I am familiar with the same phenomenon in other areas. The history of art and aesthetics recalls the history of religion: the same proclamations, exclusions, coteries, illuminati.

---

*Here he laughed for the first time – a direct, spontaneous laugh that would often return. It was as if he had another hidden personality which suddenly manifested itself.

For example, when a film comes out, or a book, or a play we often know in advance what this or that critic is going to say. No need to read his article, whether favourable or hostile. The article wasn't prompted by the work itself, but by the person who wrote it – and often without the person's knowing it.

Yes, people are like that.

It seems to me that Buddhism offers a different path, a particular form of tolerance. Might it have an easier time than other traditions in adapting itself to the evolution of times and customs? Might it also offer help to men and women less educated than others, less cultured, less intelligent?

In Buddhism everything is often a matter of the level, or the angle of approach. All general and definitive affirmations seem dangerous to us, and probably false. You ask me: now that the century is ending, can Buddhism provide a refuge for everyone? That depends on your attitude and your needs. In any case you have to distinguish between being inside or outside the structure.

Being in the structure means belonging to a Buddhist community?

Exactly. Belonging to the Sangha, accepting a particular study and discipline.

Is that possible for everyone, even outside of Asia?

Of course. Unlike Hinduism, Buddhism has always had a vocation for universality. It has opposed the gods who protect only one people, gods whose power stops at certain frontiers. Buddhism addresses all women, all men, all beings. But notice:

not on the same level, not in the same way. Those who wish to adhere to the Sangha have to act with great prudence. This is a very serious decision, which takes up a whole lifetime, or even several lifetimes. You don't renounce your past and your roots with impunity. And in any case, we do nothing to convert people. That's not our goal.

The very notion of an apostolic mission, of those vast conversion operations, so briskly carried out in the nineteenth century and even in the twentieth, seems to be on the way out.

No need to complain about that.

And the second level?

The second level is accessible to everyone. Lessons, teachings of every kind can be drawn from Buddhism without having to adhere to it completely. Buddhism can teach you tolerance, without which no life is bearable, and the path to peace of mind, which is indispensable to every just action. Peace of mind is at the center of our research. It determines our attitude toward the world we are part of, toward our neighbours, and also toward our enemies.

Are there techniques for achieving?

Of course. The main one is meditation, which is at the core of our practice, and forms part of our teaching.

We all know that a moment of quiet reflection can help us resolve a problem that seems impossible. I've found that even to be true on a group level. A few minutes of common silence can bring more cohesion to a group than hours of agitation can. But in preparing a show you can't be content with meditating. You have to get into the game, into improvisation, and the expression of vitality.

That's true everywhere. You have to meditate and play, both at once! And all together. And eat too! We have so many things in common! Water, oxygen!

One of the things that meditation teaches us, when we slowly descend into ourselves, is that the sense of peace already exists in us. We all have the deep desire for it even if it's often hidden, masked, thwarted. Buddhists believe that human nature, if we examine it carefully, is good, well disposed, helpful. And it seems to me – in response again to your first question – that nowadays the spirit of harmony is increasing, that our desire to live together calmly is growing stronger and stronger; it's more and more widespread.

But the West, as this century ends, finds itself bankrupt. A great hope arose two or three centuries ago, at the beginning of the era we call 'modern times'. Philosophers such as Rousseau also proclaimed the goodness and innocence of human nature. They thought its corruption was due to life in society. This is the corruption that Buddhists call 'contamination'.

For different reasons.

They believed and affirmed that by changing the conditions of life in society they could restore to human nature its pristine qualities, and lead people to a better life – even to happiness. More than two centuries have now passed. In that time immense social and political struggles have unquestionably allowed us to improve considerably our judicial systems, life expectancy, and standard of living. In principle, everyone in our democracies now has a chance. The state is separated from religious authorities, and justice from political power. This, however, has not been without its rough spots. At the moment we are going through an obstinate economic crisis, but on the whole we are living better, much better than we did before.

Without a doubt.

And yet human nature doesn't seem to have changed a bit.

Perhaps it's better known.

Perhaps. And better maintained by rules. But oftentimes it shows itself to be the same. In the West, religions have lost their dominance; the political ideologies have at the very least deteriorated. But happiness is still far off; and we are, when all is said and done, quite sadly the same.

I would add that in the face of this disarray racist anathemas and fundamentalism of every stripe are finding fertile soil.

Whoever excludes others will find himself excluded in turn. Those who affirm that their God is the only God are doing something dangerous and pernicious, because they are on the way to imposing their beliefs on others, by any means possible.

And to proclaiming themselves the chosen people.

Which is the worst of all.

Democracy thought it had established a strong barrier by putting into practice the very important idea of separation.

If you are referring to the separation of Church and State, that strikes me as an excellent principle.

Yet you yourself are an example to the contrary, since you unite all the power in your own hands.

No! The very notion of power is quite different. The tide itself, the institution of the Dalai Lama, could disappear overnight. It wasn't established forever by some force outside human beings and the earth. There's no contradiction between Buddhism and democracy.

Another separation you already know – the one that defines and separates the powers within the state. It could be said that the decision to make justice a power, a real power, was a stroke of genius by the West. Even if this separation stirs up all sorts of friction.

To return to fundamentalism, to the fragmentation of beliefs, to the self-styled 'chosen peoples', this is no doubt one of the reasons why Buddhism has always shied away from affirming the existence and omnipotence of a creator god. When asked about that point and several others, the Buddha Sakyamuni kept silent.

Didn't he say that we must avoid 'courting strange gods'?

He did. And all the Buddhist schools agree on that point today. Which doesn't mean, by the way, that we have rationalized our beliefs, in the sense you give that word.

We recognize the existence of superior beings, or at least of a certain superior state of being. We believe in oracles, omens, interpretations of dreams, reincarnation. But these beliefs, which for us are certainties, are not something we try to impose on others in any way. I repeat: we don't want to convert people. Buddhism's main attachment is to the facts. It's an experience, a personal experience even. Recall the celebrated saying by Sakyamuni: 'Expect everything from yourselves.'

I am also reminded of the Buddha's recommendation: 'As you test gold by rubbing it and cutting it and melting it, so judge my words. If you accept them, don't let that be out of mere respect.'

On a slightly different subject, I would like to ask you about aggression. Can we extrapolate from a long and patient study of animal behaviour? Can we say that aggressiveness is a constituent part of our nature? This notion is sometimes presented as a positive force, as an element of survival. Without it we might have disappeared.

Aggression is an intimate part of ourselves. That is why we have to struggle. Men raised in a strictly nonviolent environment have managed to become the most horrible butchers. This proves that the most insane aggressiveness continues to live in the depths of us. There's no doubt about that.

But our true nature is calm. That is why Sakyamuni advises us to search deeply in ourselves: because we will ultimately find there the desire for peace. We all know that the human mind is agitated, subject to frightful jolts. But this agitation isn't the dominant force. It's possible and necessary to master it. In your work as a screenwriter, when you imagine stories and scenes, don't you need clam?

I need both calm and agitation.

At the same time?

Almost at the same time.

So a certain agitation is needed for invention?

In the twentieth century many writers have enjoyed working, for example, in cafes, amid noise and movement, in contact with different kinds of life. After this you certainly need long moments of tranquility and reflection. The calm judges the agitation. But each person must find his or her own rhythm and manner. There's no absolute rule.

So you need a constant coming and going?

In a way. Everything begins with our little internal theater, where characters appear. We are at once actors, spectators, and even critics. From time to time one has to throw oneself completely, almost blindly, into the scene. At other times you have to distance yourself from it and look at it from far away, as if somebody else had written it.

As a screenwriter and author, it's impossible for me to live permanently on good feelings. I have to search in myself for the vicious and the criminal. In a writer's work the sin of intention doesn't exist, and when he searches in his depths, he doesn't find calm, but, on the contrary, he finds competition, violence, and often blood. He is by necessity an inventor of crimes.

At least he doesn't commit them.

Some say that he incites the spectators to commit them.

I know what you're talking about, and it does not have a simple answer. It may surprise you, perhaps, but I'm not strictly opposed to the spectacle of violence and crime. It all depends on the lessons you draw from it.

At the very heart of Buddhist tradition the attitude it constantly recommends in our relations with a reality often characterized as 'relative' ('Come to know suffering, even though there is nothing to know…') has a lot in common with a *game*. By their very condition, humans are obliged to live in a world whose reality is not assured and which may be an illusion. Thus they are like actors who identify (or seem to identify) with a role, which, like all roles, is feeling.

A third reason for optimism is that when I meet young people, especially in Europe, I sense that the concept of *humanity as one* is much stronger nowadays than it once was. You know, it's a new feeling that seldom existed in the past. The 'other' was the barbarian, the one who was different.

The one you can't recognize as being like you.

Exactly. And I see that this reaction of mistrust and hostility is slowly wearing away. We give less and less importance to nationalities, to frontiers. The unification of a large part of Europe, the disappearance, for example, of the horrible battles between the French and the Germans, the increasing number of marriages between women and men of different countries, of different languages and cultures – all that seems positive to me. A global view of things is developing, don't you think?

What you say is unquestionable. Still, what about our persistent anxieties, and the paradoxes that attack us? We have never manufactured so many goods, and yet destitution is at our gates. Never have we so frenetically multiplied our species, despite the deserts gaining ground every day. We have never seemed so close to a golden age of harmonious idleness, and now unemployment becomes our supreme scourge. Never have we so widely flaunted our bodies and our sexuality and never has death been so close to sex. Never have we invented such prodigious techniques for making contact with one another, and yet solitude has never had more bitter accents. The list goes on.

All that is true. But nothing can be settled in a hurry, as if by magic. You need time, there has to be slow progress in people's minds. Look at this, for example: in the first part of this century the inhabitants of the earth had no sense of responsibility toward their planet. Bit by bit factories covered the earth, especially in the West, dumping their wastes into all the elements. For some strange reason nobody paid any attention to this. This resulted in a massive wave of extinction of species, the most terrible we've known in 65 million years. For a Buddhist this is a perfect abomination.

The extinction continues worse than ever.

I know. But at least today we've gotten some awareness of this danger. We've even seen the formation of political parties, often called 'Greens', whose platform is built on defending the environment. Thirty or forty years ago, this first step was inconceivable. Another thing, more and more frequently I meet groups of businessmen who once upon a time, as you can well imagine, never showed any interest in Buddhism; but now they come to meet us and ask questions. They show a keen interest in our values. They even look for places to meet or make a retreat, to lead a spiritual life under our direction, at least for a week or two.

Isn't it too late?

I hope not. And in any case it's better than nothing. We always run a greater risk of losing touch with the rest of the universe.

We must do everything to maintain those ties and even to reinforce them.

Sometimes you can appease your conscience in a one-or-two-week retreat, and then immediately launch out again into frantic exploitation of the earth.

I know.

Might we need an awakening?

That's the word. That's exactly the word.

2

Education and Contamination

At the age of twenty-nine, Prince Siddhartha, already married and a father, left the splendid palace where he had lived since birth, surrounded by flowers and perfumes, and by men and women carefully chosen by his father for their youth and beauty. He walked down the streets of the city of Kapilavastu, where first he met an old man, then a man stricken by the plague, and finally a cadaver being carried to the funeral pyre.

These three encounters – the sudden revelation of old age, sickness, and death, calamities common to us all – led the prince to leave home shortly afterwards. Intrigued by a meeting with a begging monk, Siddhartha Gautama secretly left his palace, his family, and the royal duties that awaited him. He decided to concentrate all the energies of his life to seeking out a hitherto unknown new light that would permit human beings to free themselves from the inevitable suffering that he had just seen for himself.

Suffering is the revelation of Buddhism. This, of course, includes physical suffering, but also moral suffering, the feeling of impotence, frustration, and uselessness in this world. For the

Buddha, suffering 'is being born, aging, falling sick, being tied to what one does not love, being separated from what one does love, not realizing one's desire.'

To seek a remedy for this essential suffering (*dukha* in Sanskrit) Siddhartha wandered over parts of India, questioned men with a reputation for wisdom, and spent six years in the mountains where he wore himself out with extreme asceticism. It was all in vain.

He ultimately found the answer in himself, while seated on a patch of grass beneath a fig tree. This world, which grows old and dies, and is then reborn only to grow old and dies once again, is wretched. That was the first truth. Seeking the cause of this wretchedness he found birth and the desire for birth: 'At the origin of this universal pain lies the thirst for existence, the thirst for pleasures that the five external senses experience along with the internal sense, and even the thirst to die.'

Thus suffering comes from desire. That was the second truth. Such desire is like a fire inflaming the one who desires. Everything is on fire, the Buddha says again, the eye is on fire, what it sees is on fire, what the ear hears is on fire, everything that touches the senses is on fire. Illusion devours us like a permanent flame. And this fire of life, ignited by lust, anger, and ignorance, must be extinguished.

Later on Siddhartha Gautama, having become the Buddha (meaning 'the Enlightened One') added two more truths to the first two. It is possible, he said, to put out the fire and thus come to the cessation of all suffering. And lastly, the fourth revelation is that there exists a specific path to that cessation, and he pointed it out.

These teachings constitute 'the four noble truths', which are the point of departure and the very foundation for all Buddhist research.

Another important concept the Dalai Lama touches on in our discussion is the idea of the interdependence of all things. It flies in the face of everything we think we know, of our analytic vision of the world as divided into separate objects: my hands, the pen that it holds, the paper I write on, the table the paper rests on, the house that contains the table ... None of these objects has a separate existence, nor can they be considered by themselves.

Interdependence (*Paticca Samuppada* in Pali) was taught by the Buddha himself, particularly in the *Avatamsaka* Sutra. This sutra tell us that it's impossible to find any object not related to all the others.

In his book *The Heart of Understanding*, contemporary Zen master Thich Nhat Hanh uses a simple sheet of paper as an example to illustrate this idea of interbeing. Everything has some connection with this sheet of paper. If we follow all the constituent elements to their source – the wood pulp to the tree, the tree to the forest, the forest to the lumberjack, the lumberjack to his father and mother, and so on – we find that in reality the sheet of paper is empty. It has no separate self. It is made up entirely of nonpaper elements, and is empty of an independent identity. Empty in this sense, Thich Nhat Hanh tells us, means that the paper is full of all things, full of the entire cosmos.

Needless to say, what holds true for a sheet of paper also holds true for an individual. We are each made of nonindividual elements. Thich Nhat Hanh also tells us that when we meditate, we are in no way cutting ourselves off from the rest of the world. The suffering that the meditating individual transports into his or her heart is society itself. When we meditate we do it for all beings. We do it even for things that are incapable of meditating. To echo an ancient saying, we are not at the very heart of ecology itself.

The incomparable awakening which the Buddha himself achieved came from a man whose intelligence and tenacity strike us today as prodigious. (Even if the stories of his life are strongly flavoured with legends, no one seems to doubt his historical existence and the authenticity of his preaching.) This revelation assumes that all the other men and women to whom the Buddha would deliver his teaching during the next forty-five years were living in ignorance and consequently in suffering. We may think ourselves happy, we may sing at the top of our lungs that life is beautiful, we may believe we know something about the world, even presume to teach others about it. But as long as the internal awakening, the fruit of a strictly personal experience, has not been granted us, we will be living in ignorance. It is our nature and our prison, and everything must be done to destroy it.

Yet this awakening cannot be taught; the road that takes us there has to be shown to us. That is why throughout the history of Buddhism, teaching has occupied a decisive, central place. Today, in Dharamsala, the Tibetans are justifiably proud of their schools, and the Dalai Lama has made great personal effort to create a Tibetan university. Students come from all over to receive a Buddhist education from the monks. Though Buddhist, the curriculum is also quite up-to-date, and the Dalai Lama himself uses the university to keep up with the latest scientific research. He is hungry for information, and says he is learning every day.

In the ideas above there may seem to be a slight contradiction: human nature is good, but it is also subject to an undeserved ignorance and wretchedness. For a Buddhist this contradiction isn't a contradiction at all. It is the core expression of our condition; it's up to us to get ourselves out of it.

Moderating his optimism somewhat from the previous conversation, the Dalai Lama admits that we are going through a critical period. For this period he insists on education.

Our whole educational system is in a crisis. It can't adapt. In fact this crisis extends to industry and politics. Everything seems to be escaping our thought, and hence our control.

How should we react?

As always, in two ways. We can let ourselves drift into discouragement and quickly be swamped by egoism. We can tell ourselves: All is lost, times are getting harder, the world no longer knows where it's going. It's the Kali Yuga taking over, after all. So let's retreat into our corner, let's profit from the little good we may have accumulated, let's forget the rest, and then we'll see.

I know people who live like that.

Oh, me too!

And the other attitude?

It's a very simple act of awareness and precise commitment. Awareness of our condition, of the thousand dangers that hem us in. A clear commitment to getting ourselves out, an attitude that strikes me as more necessary today than ever. Human beings have to wake up.

What are we waiting for?

Nothing can get done abruptly. The real changes are slow and invisible. For example, it seems to me that the attraction the West has felt toward Buddhism for some years now is tied in with two particular notions, which have nothing spectacular about them, but which are very deeply felt. The first is *ahimsa*, nonviolence, which is gradually becoming an established force. The second is the notion of *interdependence,* which has been a part of Buddhist thought from time immemorial.

And which is bound up with our ecological concerns?

The concept of the independent existence of living creatures and things has always been rejected, from the first, in the very words of the founder by practically all Buddhist schools. Nothing exists separately. On the contrary, everything is connected to everything else, as is being explained in the Questions of Net of Indra Sutra. No species – not even the human species – can place itself outside the world, outside the wheel of the universe. We are one of the cogs in that wheel.

A wheel that's squeaking louder and louder.

You've said that we are going through a crisis, you've even said that time is pressing. Are you troubled by the population explosion of the twentieth century?

Very troubled. It's an extremely important problem.

Maybe problem number one.

Yes, I think so. Since 1987, the population has passed 5 billion. Seven or eight hundred million people have been added since that date. In less than thirty years, this global figure may double.

A 1992 forecast by UNESCO points to spectacular increases: China and India will reach $1^1/_2$ *billion each, Nigeria will become the third most populous country in the world. At this moment the population of the earth is growing by more than 90 million people a year. Another Mexico every twelve months! What can we do?*

First of all, people have to be clearly informed, without hypocrisy, without prejudice. We have to say clearly: 6 billion inhabitants is too much. Morally it's a grave error, because of the aggravated distortion between the rich countries and the poor countries. And as a practical matter it's frightening.

That will be 7 billion tomorrow, and so on. To make a noticeable dent in a demographic progression takes at least sixty years of continuous efforts.

It's a really critical point, all the more so because the experts say the earth's resources will not be enough.

That point is debated, though. Everything depends on what you mean by 'resources'. Some calculate that the earth is capable of feeding 10 or 12 billion persons. Others even talk about 50 billion. Biogenetic agriculture makes wild promises about giant salads, inexhaustible carrots, etc.

Yes, you hear talk about it everywhere. Giving people food is something we can manage, if we succeed in reducing the omnipotence of commerce, which is far from simple. Giving them water is less certain. But in any case, is it enough to define life by saying it consists of eating and drinking?

No, of course not.

Where to find work? Things to do? Leisure? Time – and space – for solitude and meditation?

The experts hardly care about that. Nor, when they talk about 50 billion people, do they care to talk about how you stop at 50 billion. With a population figure like that, the rate of increase becomes prodigious. It isn't a Mexico every year anymore, it's an entire continent.

And what to say about the growing gap between the rich countries and the poor countries? Even as far back as the beginning of the eighteenth century that gap was already there. At that time some European countries were five times richer than African or Asian kingdoms. But in the twentieth century, by the '60s, that gap had become 80 to 1. Today it would be 300 or 400 to 1, still in favour of the West, if you add on Japan.

And it doesn't stop growing. For the rich more riches, for the poor more poverty.

The two problems are closely connected. The growth in population is very much bound up with poverty, and in turn poverty plunders the earth. When human groups are dying of hunger, they eat everything, grass, insects, everything. They cut down the trees, they leave the land dry and bare. All other concerns vanish. That's why in the next thirty years the problems we call 'environmental' will be the hardest ones humanity has to face. 'This is *absolutely* the case.'

I'll give you a simple example. Years back when I drove along the road to the airport or somewhere else, I never saw chickens in the streets, in the shop fronts of stores or restaurants. Now I see them everywhere. Although it's impossible to be a total vegetarian in Tibet, I find killing animals repugnant. As far as possible I eat only vegetables and fruits. But why these rows of slaughtered chickens? Why else except because of an excessive human population? The more numerous man is, the more he kills.

Another key, obviously, is money, the stubborn quest for money, by the rich out of greed, by the poor out of necessity. Money is also why animals are slaughtered. But I put overpopulation at the root of all the dangers, of all the threats of which we've been speaking.

So you are for birth control?

Absolutely. It has to be publicized and promoted.

Some religious traditions are opposed to it.

That's right, even within Buddhism. But it's time to break down those barriers.*

Let's look at our attitude toward human life, since that's the issue. Even though subject to suffering, human life, in our eyes, is a precious phenomenon, because of the intelligence that animates us and that can rise in quality. From this standpoint birth control is pernicious, because it prevents human lives from existing.

From an individual point of view.

Exactly. Each individual is a marvellous opportunity. And abortion is a violent act, which we reject. But if we look at things from a certain distance, if we make an effort (which isn't easy) to achieve a global viewpoint, then we see quite simply that there are too many of us for this planet. And tomorrow that overload is going to get worse. Now it's no longer a matter of self-satisfied fascination with the complex beauty of our minds; it's really a

---

* The Dalai Lama paused for a few moments of reflection here; it was clear that this is an issue which he has much considered.

matter of survival. At this moment we number more than 5 billion precious lives on earth. These 5 billion precious lives find themselves directly threatened by other precious lives, to which we are adding millions and millions more.

So it's not just human life that's threatened.

Of course not. The wild animals, the trees, everything has to give way to our precious lives. In Tibet deforestation has been fierce for the past thirty years. This had led, as it does everywhere, to the impoverishment of the land. And most of the wild animals that I admired in my childhood have vanished. You know well how many species have been annihilated by the spreading of our precious life!

So if we want to defend life, and more particularly the 5 billion precious lives now pressing on the planet, if we want to give them a little more prosperity, justice, and happiness, we have to forbid ourselves to go on multiplying. Isn't that logical?*

Human life is composed of nonlife elements and in no way can it be separated from the rest of the world. It isn't 'different'. If it has value in our eyes, that value can only be relative and always connected to the mind. It is a major error, a 'root-error', to isolate human life, to attribute to it an essence, an in-itself. Then

---

* It is unfortunate that this voice couldn't get a hearing at the U.N. Cairo conference on the world's population in September 1994, because he wasn't invited. On the occasion of that gathering, which the Dalai Lama judged 'very important', the traditional rigorous positions were once again loudly proclaimed: the refusal to see the world as it is, the imposition of silence and submission on women, the defense of fidelity and abstinence, that is, the absence of love.

But at least – and this is also the Dalai Lama's opinion, at our meeting in September – the problem of overpopulation has been raised in public, and some fair-minded statements were made.

there is the fear that as the result of declining awareness, which is always possible, individual humans may no longer find the energy, the quality of mind, necessary for the next incarnation.

In the early '90s, Europe was recovering from several years of drought. The rainfall pattern did eventually become normal again, but in the dry period we had blindly paved over the earth at many points in various construction projects. In doing so we had radically changed the methods for distributing water so that it could now only stream over the earth, without soaking in to the ground. As a result we had a series of floods in 1993 and 1994. It's ridiculous to accuse heaven of unleashing these catastrophes, since here we are the only guilty parties.

Some fifteen years ago, I found myself in Mexico, during the first visit of Pope John Paul II. On the eve of his arrival, a doctor friend had invited me to dinner. When I got to his house and rang the bell, the woman who answered the door was crying. As I walked in, I was surprised to see a number of people (some of them doctors) with a downcast look. Two or three others were weeping. I asked them why they were so sad. My friend told me, 'Didn't you hear what he announced in his first speech?' 'Who?' I asked. 'The Pope.'

What did he say?

What he says everywhere: 'Mexican men and women, you must have all the children that God sends you!' With a few phrases, this old man, a professional celibate, had just destroyed ten years of patient efforts on the part of those men and women of goodwill to introduce some basic elements of contraception into a country reeling from what American ecologists call the population bomb. This group of doctors had to begin all over again.

On the other side of the coin, in 1992 I found myself in Iran, an Islamic country, which we call fundamentalist, and to my great amazement I saw on the official government channel a TV show, presented by women, explaining and recommending contraception.

In Iran?

Yes. And I think the same thing exists in Egypt. It's the kind of information that the West doesn't like to broadcast. On that point we are behind the times.

In the United States, just as in Europe, we're even seeing a return to what you call the 'moral order'.

That's right. A return to censorship, to convulsive agitation by people who, for example, oppose abortion, a violent act, by even more violent acts. As if they wanted the impossible, namely to go backwards. Could it be that life has become the enemy of life?

Human life, yes. Since it threatens all life.

On this point traditional thinking is scarcely any help.

No, because it dates from a time when human life was rare and much sought after. Many kinds of dangers lay in wait for it. Infants died at a young age. Today everything has changed, especially in the last fifty years.

What can we say about what the genetics of the next century promise? Cloning – the easy duplication of any human being – leads to the ultimate dream of immortality.

Yes, but this easy, accurate reproduction implies that we are putting an end to our evolutionary possibilities. We declare that we're perfect, and we stop there. And, on the other hand, if we do attain immortality, that is if we suppress our death, by the same token we will have to suppress birth, because the earth would become too rapidly overburdened.

Everywhere you look the simple prolonging of the average human life poses insoluble problems. How should one treat these new old people? Keep them busy? Pay their pensions?

Yes. What to do with immortality, then? In our relations with life, the change is radical. The change in our thinking, and consequently in our attitudes, has to be just as radical.

You're not strictly attached to the letter of your Scriptures?

On the contrary. You'd have to be crazy to maintain them with all your might in a world swept away by the movement of time. For example, if science shows that the Scriptures are mistaken, the Scriptures have to be changed.

For centuries the Catholic Church fought a long and sterile fight to safeguard the historical truth of the Bible, even in the face of scientific discoveries. That must seem absurd to you?

Useless, in any case, since Buddhism tells us exactly the opposite. It's a central theme, which all the schools accept: we are haphazardly plunged into impermanence. Like the essence of beings, stability of Scriptures is an illusion. Reality slips between our fingers, and we can't hold onto it.

Does that feeling arise from the certitude that we have of our death?

No, because death is simply a passage from one state to another. It's a matter of a dissolution and recomposition *at every instant.* The world goes on. Nothing fixed; nothing permanent remains. The Scriptures, venerable and sacred as they are, are relative and impermanent, like all things.*

In that case, was the Buddha also dependent on everything that surrounded him?

Of course. It's not as if he alone of us all enjoyed a miraculously autonomous life. He too was made up of non-Siddhartha elements. And it was and is the same for his thought.

Is that where the flexibility of Buddhist tradition comes from?

That flexibility, as you call it, comes above all from experience. It's true, our experience is very old and very rich. It has allowed

---

* This is certainly a point in Buddhism that at first surprises and then attracts us. In the monotheistic religions that constitute our tradition we are used to Scriptures revealed, now by God now by one of his angels or prophets. In any event, they come from somewhere else. The man who proclaimed them or wrote them down was nothing but the spokesman of a supposed beyond. It was, it still is in many cases, out of the question, unimaginable, to modify, ever so slightly, a saying held to be strictly divine.

There is no such thing in Buddhism. It must be repeated that the Buddha drew his four fundamental truths and all the teaching that followed from deep within himself. He never stopped saying that this teaching had to be meticulously verified at every moment by experience, and by personal experience at that. Even though in certain currents of Buddhism and in Hinduism (which saw in Siddhartha the ninth avatara of Vishnu, after Krishna), Buddha has sometimes been enlisted in the ranks of the gods, he remains today a human being.

us, time and again, to measure the dangers of isolation, the uselessness of dogmatic authority, the vanity of fundamentalism. I repeat, first we establish the facts, at any rate those that are unquestionable, like the increase in the population. Then we try to analyze the causes that have brought on these facts, and the conditions in which they arose – without losing sight for an instant of interdependence and impermanence. Finally, if necessary, we change our attitude.

Reflecting from an ancient point of view can help us. Apart from experience, this supplies us with both doctrine and distance. Very often we go astray in the chaos of present-day life. If we look at our world from too close up, we can't see it anymore. It's good to start out again, every day, from far away.

But can that permanent recourse to tradition also close our eyes?

Naturally. It can paralyze us. We must above all remain open and sensitive. Then, if we have the means, we have to show others what must be done. It's certain that the old religious prohibitions sometimes harm us. But how to bend them? With what weapons?

The countless representations of the Buddha that have followed one another in various countries are based on a complicated symbolism. The position of his body, its five different levels, his particular physical characteristics, such as the long ears, the broad shoulders, the cranial bulge, all have meaning. The sculptors and painters have paid special attention to his hand positions, which are called *mudras*. Among the eight *mudras* there is one called 'preaching' (*Dharmachakra mudra*): both hands, one with the palm turned outward, the other inward, the index fingers and the thumbs touching, show the wheel of dharma, that is, of the world order. This really is a wheel, and it never stops turning. It's futile to whatever may be our stubborn insistence on building, our fascination with stability, our 'hard desire to hold on', this gesture is here to remind us of the movement which controls all things. The Buddha felt and expressed this perfectly. Immobility is an illusion, and our body serves as the best example of that. It never ceases, every split second, to break down. The last words of the Awakened one were accompanied by a gesture pointing to his wrecked body, the victim of a bloody dysentery: 'Everything composite is vowed to destruction.'

His successors embroidered at leisure on this theme, and in so doing have influenced related schools of thought. We find, for example, a perfectly Buddhist phrase within a sixth-century hymn to Shiva: 'The unmoved is dispersed/And the moving remains.'

The Dalai Lama himself has often spoken about impermanence, about the continuous changes that phenomena undergo. He even finds confirmation of this in the incessant motion of subatomic particles. Our consciousness also has but a momentary existence. What remains, what's always there, is what Buddhists call the 'sixth mental consciousness', the deepest one, which has neither beginning nor end, and which transcends the usual categories of time and space. We will return to this 'subtle consciousness' at some length when we speak about the mind.

Even if this subtle consciousness can undergo passing change, even if the most radical schools claim it can't escape the universal illusion that beguiles us, in a certain fashion its 'continuity endures'. In the same way, amid the many upheavals of our day-to-day existence, a sort of continuity subsists, that of human society. But this continuity is the underpinning of change, without it we couldn't perceive change to begin with.

Sometimes it seems to me that the Pope would like to stop the wheel of this world. Isn't the real answer given by the Buddha's silent gesture?

Undoubtedly. The Pope, which is only normal, is directly influenced by the religious traditions that he represents. Thus he becomes attached to a principle: human life being a precious good, the greatest number of people must benefit from it. But that runs counter to another principle, which is another form of respect for life, and not just human life. Yes, life *is* precious, but its quality has to be defended. So it's one principle against another. For us slavish obedience to a principle constitutes no choice at all. It seems to me that our intelligence is there precisely so that we can be flexible and adapt. Everything is relative. A blocked intelligence is not an intelligence. If I have to cut off one of my fingers to save the other nine, I don't hesitate. I cut it off.

Here or there we see men abandoning themselves to desperate, even criminal efforts, to stop movement of time, to carve out and protect a space that we say is inseparable from the rest.

Mixed in with appetites of all sorts.

That goes without saying.

From the point of view of birth control isn't China the only country that has tried a systematic policy on a grand scale?

Yes. And for a long time. Unfortunately, after the occupation of Tibet, that policy was extended to annexed territories, where the native population was still rather thinly spread. Very harsh measures were taken, going so far as forced sterilization of Tibetan women. At the same time they pursued a policy of occupying the land, by transferring Chinese populations to Tibet.

Is that a masked colonization?

Exactly. The supposed population controls, which are obligation in Tibet, as they say, just as 'in the rest of China', conceal a forced colonization, which is very effective. In the territory of the old independent kingdom of Tibet, the Chinese occupiers are today more numerous than the native Tibetans.

A passage in Nietzsche's Thus Spoke Zarathustra *occurs to me: The earth, he [Zarathustra] said, has a skin; and this skin has diseases. One of these diseases is called, for example, 'man'. That's certainly the most pessimistic vision. Can we take care of that disease?*

I hope so. But without eliminating the whole human race!

In the early 1970s, more than twenty years ago, an American doctor and engineer, James Lovelock, launched the Gaia hypothesis. It argues that our planet has borne for billions of years a very rare, perhaps even unique, phenomenon called life, with which it interacted in a special manner. The earth might have, if not a personal life, at least its own particular reactions.

Coolly received by most scientists, the Gaia hypothesis stirred up among readers a series of echoes, quite often excessive. As Lovelock himself said, to explain this success, beyond the destruction of the planet that we are witnessing (and participating in) at each moment of our existence, one has to look for some very ancient reasons. The personification of the earth, often with feminine gender, can be found on every page of our mythological accounts. In India she is called Bhumi. She is, as in other places, our mother.

In the *Mahabharata*, the immense foundational epic poem where all of India meets, a great battle throws all known peoples into ferocious conflict, and threatens the survival of the earth itself, indeed to the entire universe. In fact, on both sides the combatants possess the supreme weapon, called *Parasurama*, a burning, shinning weapon capable of annihilating all life in a few instants. Because of it the plants tremble in fear, like the rocks, like the gods.

And because of it, at a given moment, despite her pacific nature, Bhumi, the earth, joins in the battle. She seizes in 'her muddy hands' the wheel of the chariot of Karna, one of those 'arrogant men' who might call upon the fearful weapon. She blocks his chariot, resisting all human effort, and thus delivers the warrior to his death.

Even today this participation of the earth in our combats is as much longed for as it is dreaded. Some people claim, rather naïvely, that the AIDS virus is a response by 'nature' to our all-conquering proliferation, and that at this moment other viruses, with unimaginable symptoms, are bubbling away in the most secret of crucibles. While there is something infantile in such fantasies, they do in any event translate our feelings of alarm and, in a strange way, our hopes.

But the key is in our hands. We mustn't look for it anywhere else. It's true that humans are the only species with the power to destroy the earth. The birds and rabbits don't have this power. But if it has the power to destroy the earth, humanity also has the power to protect it.

It's not taking that path. The river that flows through my village in the south of France was once a place of joy, for meeting people, for bathing, fishing, irrigation. Today it's polluted and abandoned, and has been for thirty years now, dirty and shameful, assassinated.

Even here, in Dharamsala, I was surprised while walking in the forest to see piles of dirty paper, tin cans, plastic. It all seemed to have been thrown every which way.

That's the contribution of the Tibetan community?

Yesterday, near the hotel, I saw a group of Tibetan children playing very noisily. Their game consisted in pulling all the trash out of a garbage can and throwing it in all directions. I stopped, I wondered. What are they doing? Why?

They're seven or eight years old. They were born into a garbage-can world. For them nature is full of plastic. That's how it is, they never saw it the way it was before. They don't know that the world used to be beautiful. The very notion of beauty may be something they'll never experience.

Then what should we do?

All we have is education. It's our only weapon, along with the example we can set. And this education, from the Buddhist viewpoint, begins with the notion of interdependence.

Everything depends on everything else. The life of those children you saw playing is directly bound up with the dirty paper they snatch out of the garbage cans. This has to be said and explained; above all it has to be proved.

It's a long task.

Yes, an everyday task that will never be finished. But that's the price we have to pay for our survival and for the quality of our survival. This shared awareness is essential if we want to improve, however little, our own attitude toward the world, our own relationship with it. We must overcome the isolation of our mind, we must renew our ties with the rest of the universe. Otherwise we are lost. Lost because separate. We have to show people, indefatigably, that our interest is the interest of others, that our future is the future of others. And when I say 'others', I'm not thinking just of human beings, who are evidently the same as us. I'm thinking of all the other forms of life, on this earth and outside this earth.

So it's not a question of feelings, nor of morality?

It's first of all a fact.* Now the fact is that we have only one earth, that it is our common mother, and that any harm that we do

* All those who have taken an interest, whether immediate or remote, in Buddhism have been struck by this affirmation that compassion, the very foundation of conduct, is not based in any way on what we call 'feeling'. Even if we can't help it, it does not practical good to be moved to tears over our misfortunes or the misery of others.

Buddhist compassion has nothing to do with this or that particular case. It is based on a very precise sense of our belonging to the totality of the world. Venerable texts tell us that it is without cause, without heat, without it necessarily strikes back at us. If we don't pay attention to the earth, we are destroying our own future.

Can we still save it?

Of course. Beginning with birth control, which must be promoted as quickly as possible. Along with that, yes, we can clear the rives and the soil and the air we breathe. Yes, we can do it. It's up to us. And this isn't a question of feelings or morality. It's our future that's at stake.

What of other roots, ours, the ones we call Judeo-Christian, and the origin myth in Genesis where the creator god gives humans power over all living things, the fish in the water, the birds in the air, the beasts, even the animals that crawl on the earth, as well as the grasses and the trees. In this crucial story man bestows himself, in a few phrase, the undisputed possession of the whole planet. No doubt he does this in good faith, and in the name of a god who is henceforth unique.

It's hard to measure to what extent this ancient tale still influences us today. I tend to believe that that influence is subtle but deep, present in very gesture we make.

For centuries Westerners have been telling themselves that they are the crown of creation, made in the very image of God. They have wound up believing it. Our efforts to extricate ourselves from this myth, which Buddhism has never known, are slow and hard, and they always have to begin over again. Only twenty years ago

---

passion, untiring, immovable. As Jacques Bacot remarked as early as 1925, 'It is completely objective, cold, and bound up with a metaphysical concept. It is not spontaneous, but the result of long meditations. . . . It embraces all the beings caught up by their passions in the cycle of rebirths. It is universal, whereas ours is particular.'

people in the West who felt themselves an inseparable part of the wheel were very rare.

On the contrary, the majority – and this is still true – took themselves to be the ones who made the wheel turn.

Sure. You were speaking of some groups of businessmen who are here to make a retreat and who ask your advice. What are they by comparison with the millions of organized 'executives' whose only project is to exploit and further overwhelm Bhumi?

It's true that the West is fascinated by efficiency. If the problem of survival is not taken care of, there will be nobody left even to discuss the problem. And Buddhism can help here. First of all, as I said, with the enormous attention it pays to the notion of interdependence. That can never be repeated often enough. Then with the attitude that it adopts toward dogmatic truth.

Anyway, the identity of the doctor and the remedy he prescribes are of little importance. The Buddha cited the famous example of the man struck by a poisoned arrow: he doesn't want to let himself be treated until he learns the name of the man who shot him, until he knows what caste he belongs to, to what family, if he is tall or short, in what forest the arrow was cut. And so he dies before he can be cared for.

This pragmatic attitude, which presupposes a permanent challenge to our habitual ways to thinking and acting, is the backbone of Buddhism. It has both rigour and flexibility.

Even as it affirms that every event comes from a cause and brings on consequences, in the great wheel where everything is connected to everything else, Buddhism knows how to brush aside, when necessary, any theoretical speculation which might put off the care that every wound requires.

In borderline cases, Buddhism even recognizes the obscurity that envelopes certain domains. No doubt it's better to steer clear of it, as the Buddha recommends. 'Do not try to measure the immeasurable with words, any more than to plunge the cord of thought into the impenetrable…'

This teaching also depends on the level of comprehension of the disciple. The Dalai Lama returns at every opportunity to the notions of level, measure, and adaptation. Sakyamuni seems to have always mistrusted extreme positions that might be interpreted in an eternalist sense (there is an independent soul forever in existence) or, on the contrary, in a nihilistic sense (nothing exists). His pedagogical concerns have been passed on to us by one of his continuators, Maitreya. We can see here that the Enlightened One was on guard against his own prestige. He advised putting confidence in the teaching proper, not in the person of the master. He was also mistrustful of the persuasive sweetness of words, or any fine discourse, preferring exact and direct language.

Finally, it's well known that he replied to certain questions only with silence. These zones left in shadow, where the cord of thought does not penetrate, are called 'the fourteen unexplained views'.

For us, Western seekers who pry about everywhere, who refuse to leave any sphere of knowledge unexplored (even if the consequences of the quest may often seem frightful), these fourteen definitively impenetrable points are a mystery and almost a scandal. God has given us everything to elucidate, even the darkness.

We find the mystery of that distant attitude, of those questions suspended right from the start, is increased by the enigma of

Buddhism itself. To our eyes, so hungry for clear order, Buddhism often appears ambiguous, on the edge of contradiction, where all tendencies can rub shoulders. Is it a religion? Is it a philosophy, or a moral teaching? These are questions without answers, almost out of place. Buddhism stubbornly resists being categorized; in the final analysis it has something ungraspable about it. Some minds might be repelled by this (can we conceive of problems with no solution?), by contrast, others might stroll at ease in this domain. All those who practice Buddhism insist on the necessity of experience, which resolves the theoretical doubts with the inexplicable grace of life itself.

Might our relationship to the earth pose one of those insoluble problems? Might this be a fifteenth 'unexplained view'?

The most troubling thing is that some of my friends, intelligent and cultivated people, seem incapable of seeing. It even seems that for some of them an accumulation of knowledge swells their self-confidence and blinds them, instead of alerting them. Nothing is more disturbing than the debates among scientists who refuse to make a pronouncement, when you cite the case, for example, of the ozone layer. They always need one last detail, one minor calculation. Time is pressing; as you say, the poison from the arrow is doing its job, and they don't speak out. Meanwhile the situation is clear: you run no risk in protecting the earth, even supposing that it isn't in any danger.

In the contrary case, if we do nothing, all fears are permitted.

It's pure logic. It's absolutely necessary to bet on the worst-case scenario. But people listen, nod their heads, they say: yes, yes, you're right….

And right away they forget.

As for the the political parties that call themselves ecological, they sometimes tear themselves to pieces.

Yes. The taste for power creeps in everywhere.

It's still one of the questions that troubles us: should ecology be content with action on its own turf, or should it raise itself, at the risk of being corrupted, to the political level where the decisions are made? We don't all have the same answer.

Not even the same question, I'm sure.

I read with pleasure in one of your books that you turn off the lights whenever you leave your hotel room.

That's true. I know that this gesture doesn't relieve the earth except in the smallest degree. Still, you have to begin somewhere. Begin with yourself, while hoping that a few others around you will imitate you, and that the circle will get wider. Electricity, which makes us forget the ancient fear of night, has become too familiar. There are very few young people in Europe or the United States who turn out the lights when they leave a room.

They haven't known night, the world in the dark, the sharp glow of a candle.

They're like those children who have never seen the earth clean and beautiful.

And don't forget that this ignorance makes the fortunes of those who produce electricity.

I'm not an expert in education, actually I'm ignorant in that area. But I know that the real answer is there. Our forms of education change despite us. In the West it's clear that television is in the process of taking the place of the teachers of another day. Is this good? Is it evil?

I'm also told that the young people, in the United States and even in Europe, are behaving in ways that are increasingly egotistical and cruel. I hear about the troubles in the inner city, of drug-addicted youths, of rocks thrown down on cars from highway overpasses killing people, and even of murders committed by children. Is this the result of a general decadence, of the economic crisis? Or does the daily spectacle of violence stir up our own violence.

Here's a curious fact, for example: I find that the young Tibetans who were born and have grown up in India are gentler than the ones from Tibet. They're from the same people, the same culture. They both speak the same language, and still they're different. It's the effect of the environment, I imagine.

And yet India isn't an especially peaceful country.

Who knows? Think about it. I know very well that there are problems in India, and even bloodshed. But on the whole, in India, different peoples, who speak around sixty different languages and who practice all sorts of religions, manage to coexist. Isn't that an example that the whole planet could follow? Don't blacken the picture too much. You crossed the Punjab in coming here. Once troubled, that state is now at peace. It has recovered its wealth. And think of the young Tibetans who at this moment in Tibet have to face the pressure of the Chinese occupation. There you have, no doubt, the first reason for their aggressiveness: a life without happiness, a life constantly being called into question. The systematic oppression leads them to dissatisfaction and then, very quickly, to aggression.

We all lack something. I don't know exactly what, but I sense it. In the West you have everything. At least you think you do. Even if at the moment you're going through a crisis. All the material goods are there, no doubt better parceled out than in the past. In any case, you often pride yourself on that. But it seems to me that you are living in a state of incessant tension, competition, and fear. Those who grow up in that atmosphere will always lack something, all through their life.

What will they lack?

Our most profound, most agreeable, and most fruitful dimension. They'll remain on the troubled surface of the sea, without knowing the calm they're resting on.

The Dalai Lama came to the West for the first time in 1973. The knowledge he can have of our conditions of life, and of the state of our thought, may be as limited as ours when we return from a trip to India or China. All reality is complex and changing. When he summarily characterizes the West as mechanistic and mercantile, he doesn't always avoid clichés. It's not true by a long shot that those who live in the West benefit from all the supposed comfort, from all the wonders of technology. That famous tension, that haste, that pitiless competition are not without broad openings in the clouds, without real beaches of well-being. We too have our disinterested seekers, our benefactors, our dreamers. We even have our hermits.

Thus it has to be admitted that when he speaks about the West the Dalai Lama is sometimes content, for convenience's sake, to stick with an image that has no nuances. We regularly do the same when we speak of the Arab countries, of Africa, or Japan: we keep only the striking features that simplify everything. Yet Buddhism keeps teaching us that every simplification, if indeed it claims to describe a whole society, is false and hence dangerous.

When we move on to discuss the changes that we have observed in the course of our lives, I start by mentioning a celebrated book which was one of the touchstones of the 1960s.

Margaret Mead's The Generation Gap, *was influential in that time since it recapitulated the most widespread ideas from those years, and also because it asked real questions. In traditional societies, Mead says, the world didn't change from one generation to another, or changed only a little. Thus the old people could pass on to the young, to the newcomers in the group, everything they knew about their environment, about their way of life, their tools, their stories, their social bonds. In an unchanging world new generations would have need of that knowledge. In modern times, when things began to change with increasing speed, the divergence between the generations became marked, and then got even worse. It became a deep rift. The newcomers wondered why the old people insisted on passing on this or that technology, on making them read this or that author, when another author bored them, and they no longer had any use for that technology.*

Ever since the end of the '60s our educational system has hesitated. On the one hand, the old citadels of knowledge were collapsing. A whole world of the past suddenly seemed useless to us. Latin slipped into oblivion, and mathematics picked up the slack. Teaching now announced that it was open, flexible, 'light', practically optional. In some cases the students were asked what they wanted to study.

This attitude led to a strange, almost topsy-turvy, pedagogy, which nearly produced two generations of ignoramuses. After which the usual reaction occurred, and so on.

At this moment we are still hesitating. As you say, we are well aware that the whole system has to change. But in what direction? Opinions vary.

In the airports or train stations when the police want to discover secret shipments of things, they use specially trained dogs. And it often works, because the dogs have much sharper noses than the police. But that doesn't mean that the police have to take the dogs as their professors.

I really wonder if the change has accelerated. What change? A change in what? In technology, yes. All our tools have been perfected. Some of them are new, requiring a new kind of know-how. Our clothes, or yours at any rate, are changing in accordance with the fashion. The means of transportation are being perfected, our perception of the world, our beliefs are changing, because we all live in impermanence. In external appearance things do change, they undergo endless modification.

But we, we haven't changed.

3

Not Me, Not God

Based on personal experience, having nothing to do with any divine revelation, Buddhism denies any independent existence of the 'me'. This is a unique paradox in the history of thought: what all traditions call the 'soul' (*atman* in Sanskrit), that permanent entity believed to survive us, so as to know another life or a number of other lives, resisting death, sleep, and the loss of consciousness – Buddhism seeks but never finds.

Even the contemporary notions of an 'I' or an 'ego' that do not presume any survival by the soul after death, but that establish a tangible self, a definite and durable being, are energetically refuted by Buddhists. When we say, 'my body' or 'my mind', we are presuming the existence of a being, of a person, who would have to possess that body and that mind, and who would consequently be distinct from them. It's the same when we say 'my desires', 'my regrets', 'my past', 'my courage'. Buddhism can't find that being, that self, anywhere at all.

And in fact it condemns it, because it sees in this illusory belief the origin of egoism, of attachment to possession, of jealousy, pride, and ill will toward others who live in the same error. From conflicts between individuals to wars of extermination among nations, all the misfortune that troubles us is born from that absurd dream, from that sensation of being different, particular, constant.

We are, like the piece of paper, connected to all things. We can break ourselves down into a certain number of elements, our limbs, the fragments of our limbs, the atoms that make us up, the activity of our thought, but none of these elements can claim to be the totality of a self. *That* persists in escaping us.

People, Buddhism tells us, have invented two concepts to struggle against this inconsistency – one of protection, the other of conservation. The concept of protection is called 'God', the omnipotent and omnipresent father, who reassures us in our weakness. The concept of conservation is called 'the soul', which is destined to live eternally, and serves as ground for consolation in our passage from this life.

These two further 'root-errors', which we have inscribed deep within ourselves, the idea of God and the idea of the soul, are the very sign of our ignorance. These ideas are false and empty. They are 'subtle mental projections', cleverly cloaked in words. They have an almost irresistible power, because they are born of our anxiety and our need to live.

The Buddha Sakyamuni was perfectly well aware of the revolutionary aspect of this critique of customary feelings and received ideas, which made it so hard to accept. He put it this way: 'The people who are submerged by the passions and surrounded by a mass of obscurity cannot see the truth that goes *against the current*, which is sublime, profound, subtle, and difficult to understand.'

To go 'against the current' is putting it mildly, because we are all very intimately persuaded that we are particular and permanent individuals. Most of our phrases begin with *I*. In

French and sometimes even in English people say, 'Me, I . . . ' Everything tells us that we are made up of our past actions, of our present state, of our projects for the future, that changes in us occur only on the surface, that the essential, in each one of us, subsists. 'You haven't changed' is one of the phrases we hear most often.

It's enough to enter a large bookstore and count the books that explain and illustrate the problems of the self. Shelves are overflowing with them. These works are just as numerous as they are disappointing, when one plunges into them, because none of the cases described in them seems to apply to us.

In any event, these heaps of analyses won't go away tomorrow. The very architecture of modern Western law is based principally on the individual as distinct from the mass, as both precious and threatened: a perceptible and definable individual.

Buddhism stubbornly tells us that the opposite is true. No trace of substance remains in us unchanged. We live in the midst of an uninterrupted current of relations which condition our existence at every instant. We have no possibility of speaking of our self, of our being. The Buddhists can't follow Descartes in his famous 'ergo'. Nothing naturally follows from thought to being, since both are elements of the same changing stream. Instead of affirming, 'I think, therefore I am' we could say, at most, 'I think, therefore I think', or else, as Nietzsche says, 'Something is thinking'.

This dislocation of the ego is naturally accompanied by a lively critique of memory, and of the notion of the past. That feeling of continuity that every life conveys is an extra illusion, a complacent mental game. Everything that has to do with our past – which we reconstitute and modify with our thought at every instant – is an abstraction, a mental construct, like the future. We can hardly talk prudently about the present moment.

Since despite all this it must be admitted that we exist, otherwise the search for awakening becomes incomprehensible. The Buddha admits that we are made of 'five aggregates'. Without going into the details, let's call these five aggregates the components on which our presence to the world is based: the body (or material character), sensation, perception, conformation (also called constructions), and consciousness.

But the Buddha immediately says, speaking to his first five disciples: 'The body is not the Self, perception is not the self, constructions are not the Self, any more than consciousness is the Self. . . .'

Thus none of the aggregates that make us up can claim to be ourselves (even if certain schools maintain the contrary). But what if we had to choose? What if we absolutely had to have a support, something to lean on? Then, says the Buddha, it's no doubt best to take the body, because at least it subsists for a moment, whereas 'What you call mind is produced and dispersed in a perpetual process of change'.

So we have mistrust, then, with regard to our thought, total mistrust with regard to our 'soul'.

All the continuators of the Buddha, to whatever school they belong, have insisted on this point: the self is an illusion, and the true source of suffering. The Dalai Lama himself has spoken of this persistent illusion as an 'inner demon, the most deeply rooted in us. The true practitioner must be a soldier who unceasingly fights his or her inner enemies, of whom the chief is the belief in the "self", which is surrounded and followed by all the others.'

But we, we haven't changed. If we are nothing but impermanence and illusion, just a constant, ungraspable flux, what is it in us that doesn't change? Which of our component elements can we base our efforts on? What can we change in ourselves?

If sincere Catholics, who are worried about overpopulation the way you and I do, encounter an obstacle, a real obstacle, in tradition, which they can't lightly dodge, what can they do?

You mean, if they really believe in the power of truth of the Scriptures?

Yes.

That's a rare case.

Meaning. . . ?

Christian Scriptures, in most cases, seem archaic to Christians today, and are not really followed to the letter even by those who consider themselves devout. I'm speaking more about Europe. In Africa or Latin America the problem is quite different.

But nevertheless, is there some sort of opening within Catholicism?

No doubt, but it remains well hidden. When the Pope proclaims around the world that people must have all the children that God sends them, perhaps he's flattering the virility of men or somehow appeasing their fear of growing old. Many families are convinced that one more child – preferably a boy – will be a support in their old age.

I see.

It's an indirect solution. It's astute, its results would be long in coming, and it would be very difficult to put in place.

Where would you find the money? How would you distribute it?

Many other ideas are being considered by people of goodwill. We're just beginning to see an integration of ecology into business – pollution controls, biodegradable detergents, recycled paper, organically grown fruits and vegetables. With great difficulty we're getting away from the control of industry which has been a reality for more than a century. But everything has yet to be done. Nothing reassuring can be built if the size of the population isn't controlled.

I believe so, too. But you must see that the major religious leaders are, so to speak, incapable of changing their ideas. Especially if the changeover has to be brutal. The Pope, for example, in all the texts that he hands out to the Catholic faithful, indefatigably repeats the same speech, a speech that is based on very ancient beliefs. Even if he personally felt in favour of some changes (though we don't know anything about this) the institutions that he heads forbid him to say so publicly. You've got to understand: it's impossible.

What can one hope for?

Everything has to begin from what is called 'the base'. I know perfectly well – because I've spoken with them – that in Catholic religious communities among the monks and the nuns there are individuals who sense the danger, who share our ideas, who affirm the necessity of doing something as soon as possible. It's from them, and also from the faithful, that the idea of a change must begin. In other words, they have to create an atmosphere that would make change possible. That way the indispensable decisions would get much easier for their leaders.

Then there are the scientists.

Yes. The principal effort ought to come from them.

But they belong to institutions too, and most live in physical and mental comfort. Many acknowledge they have trouble speaking out.

Still they ought to speak out, and speak out loudly, put together clear statistics and broadcast them. They have to keep telling us what numbers we have to expect.

They've done it, though not very often. But once read, they are immediately forgotten. It is difficult for people to see the relevance such studies have on their lives.

But the task of the scientists isn't just to do research, it's also to inform, otherwise their research has no meaning. What is true of population is also true of the environment. If not, do you have any other ideas? Do you know any other means of helping us clear the obstacles? Could the West really change its way of life? Is that conceivable?

For the moment a lot of attention is given to economic concerns, and these problems at hand easily eclipse all others. But the remedies proposed for these problems all come out of outmoded ways of thinking. Growth and economic renewal is framed only in terms which rely on continued exploitation of an almost exhausted planet. We have no new compelling ideas to sustain us.

Do you see the European community as a source of hope?

Yes, perhaps.

The threats to the environment don't stop at the frontiers.

Nor do shifts of population. Each Western nation has hidden populations that are not always considered. In the United States, it's estimated that there are more than 20 million illegal aliens. There too, what can be done?

We have to insist, day after day, without ever getting discouraged. We have to stress the fact there are too many of us.

I'm pleasantly surprised by the insistence with which the Dalai Lama returns to the problems of population and environment. Perhaps this is a first response to the paradox of the nonself: even while vainly seeking his permanent self, the Buddha discovered the equality of all existing things – none having a privileged place – and the relationships that united them.

There's no question of denying the existence of the world, nor of ourselves. Contrary to eternalism (the permanent essence of beings beyond the stream of existence), this attitude of radical doubt would lead to nihilism, to admitting the world as a simple mental construct.

It's not that this idea lacks seductive appeal. It has even tempted some philosophers, such as the Irishman George Berkeley in his *Three Dialogues Between Hylas and Philonous*, 1713. In Berkeley's view, the world has no existence except through our perception of it.

A very large majority of Buddhist schools, however, reject this radical negation of reality. They rely on a highly affirmative phrase of Sakyamuni's: 'There does exist a not-born, not-become, not-made, non-composed; and if it did not exist, there would be no possible escape for that which is born, become, made, and composed.'

The Dalai Lama puts it in his own way: 'When I doubt that I exist, I pinch myself.'

So there's no need for concern. We exist?

Yes. Even if our knowledge of the world and of ourselves is illusory, a 'non-born', a 'not-become', exists. Without it we wouldn't exist. But we exist in a way that is at once relative (to the activity of our mind) and conditioned (by all the other existence).

It's impossible to find the self outside the body and the mind?

Impossible. But it's equally impossible to perceive and describe our relative existence – which is strictly imprisoned in a net of causes and effects – without, by the same token, perceiving the existence of all things.

From which we are inseparable.

Exactly. Our existence is in no way independent. But it is, in itself, all existences.

And that holds even for the body all by itself, as Sakyamuni says again: 'It is within our body itself, mortal as it is and only six feet long, that we find the world and the origin of the world, and the end of the world, and, in a parallel fashion, the path that leads to *nirvana*.'

Thus the ecological positions that the Dalai Lama takes are not a matter of fashion or the fruit of some late revelation in the face of obvious environmental destruction (as it has been for many). They have long been inscribed in what is the deepest and perhaps the most original part of Buddhism. It shares them with Jainism, another Indian tradition that appeared at the same moment and in almost the same place as Buddhism, and that to this day is faithful to the teachings of its founder, Mahāvīra. One essential point in these teachings is the respect for all forms of life. Thus here and there on the highways of India one meets groups of men and women dressed in white. They walk along and beg tirelessly; and they wear over the lower part of their faces a sort of band to avoid inadvertently swallowing any small insects. In the same way before sitting down they dust off their seat with a light fly swatter to remove any tiny creatures they might risk crushing.

Without venturing into such extreme attitudes, Buddhism shares the same feeling. We are not a detached part of the world, we are the world.

When he told me, 'But we, we haven't changed', the Dalai Lama wasn't alluding to any irreducible territory that we supposedly keep and protect in ourselves. His phrase had a meaning that was apparently simpler but in fact subtler and broader. What hasn't changed, he told me, is our relationship with the world. After two centuries of barrages, barricades, strikes, social conquests, dizzying technologies, ideological furors, scientific troubles, and wars great and small, we find ourselves the same, still intimately linked to what we have claimed to know and dominate. And we see with amazement the rise of a peril we didn't expect, the threat of self-destruction, which is all the harder to avert because it continually springs from our own persistent illusion.

I began to listen to the Dalai Lama differently as he picked up this thread of the conversation with increasing emphasis and conviction.

The real problem of the Third World is ignorance. Along with attachment and aversion, ignorance is one of the three *kleshas*, one of the three poisons of the mind that are the source of all mental illness. In the Third World, ignorance is no doubt the most serious one. In the West, thanks to the force of circumstance, you are beginning to realize that something has gone wrong. And in your own fashion you are organizing and fighting back.

A fight that will be worthless if it doesn't become worldwide.

Exactly. So the people of the Third World have to be educated. And it has to be done energetically, without any sentimental reticence. It's an immediate necessity, it's an emergency. They have to be told, despite all the misunderstandings it may involve: you're on the wrong track, your demographic growth is much too large, it's leading you to even more terrible poverty. It's only normal that you want to improve your standard of living. But that's not possible for everyone. On the contrary.

The countries of the North are never satisfied. They have everything, and they want still more. Other countries, such as Ethiopia, suffer from chronic want. They have nothing, and tomorrow they will have less than nothing. We have to fight this growing gap.

That ought to be our goal. Bringing the two worlds close enough to make them comparable, and if possible equal. Yes, that should be our goal. It's morally noble, and practically everything justifies it.

Isn't that a little easy to say?

Of course. But you have to begin by saying it, and saying it clearly. All the problems that you and I have been discussing, and that every individual meets with in everyday life – famine, unemployment, delinquency, insecurity, psychological deviancy, various epidemics, drugs, madness, despair, terrorism – all that is bound up with the widening gap between the peoples, which needless to say, can also be found inside the rich countries. Buddhism is absolutely explicit on this point, and our ancient experience confirms it at every instant: everything is linked together, everything is inseparable. Consequently the gap has to be reduced.

How do we do that?

You have to say, with persuasiveness and goodwill, but also with scientific precision, you have to say to the peoples of the Third World: do you want your standard of life to equal that of the northern countries? Well, begin by reducing your birthrate. Otherwise, it's useless even to try.

So we come back to that idea of education.

Information first, then education. We can't thrust it aside.

But there are so many people who have been left behind. They have no way of being heard, and are easily forgotten. And then we know that the price for raw materials, on which many countries' economics depend on, is set in the West.

I didn't say it would be easy. Far from it. I'm saying where I think we have to begin.

Anthropologist Claude Lévi-Strauss has wondered whether our form of civilization doesn't have in itself a fatal, irresistible charm.

How do?

Since industrial Europe set out to conquer the world in the eighteenth century, every culture that enters into contact with the West seems to be immediately seduced. They want to acquire our learning, technical competence, and above all the objects that we manufacture. Lévi-Strauss asks whether this seduction, which tends to make the world uniform, isn't fatal all around. A global civilization strikes him as unimaginable and even dangerous. He is not alone in feeling that cultures live only by their diversity – by comparison and confrontation. The total domination of one culture, to the detriment of others, might mean the disappearance of the idea of culture as we know it.

It seems to me that this movement is continuing, and even worsening. All the knowledge belongs to the West, which unceasingly protects and refines it.

I'm not sure I agree with you. We obviously have the impression that all the technology comes from the West, and from the countries connected to the West like Japan. But is that mechanistic civilization *intimately* bound up with the West? I don't think so.

Amazonian Indians may want a camera, and they're right. It suits them as well it does a Frenchman or a German. Just because they didn't invent and manufacture the device doesn't mean that it's foreign to them. They don't wear clothes: that doesn't mean that they're short of clothes. That's how it is, that's all.

Of course, we have to respect the local traditions and not impose anything by force. But the destitution that we meet everywhere obliges us to make certain gestures. We have to give them food, medicine, and technology too. It's impossible to do otherwise. In itself there's nothing wrong with technology. Born in the West, it has rapidly covered the entire earth. The East adapts to it easily. On certain points, for example with regard to cost, the East is even more efficient. Frankly I don't think that machinery can be *identified* with the West. It is our common property. Who knows? It could even bring us closer and blend us together.

Would it be dangerous to separate humanity into two groups solely from the technological point of view?

Obviously. Besides all human separation is dangerous. The technological criterion is no better than any other. What one person invents is good for everybody.

But there's still an attitude of superiority.

That feeling exists, it's true. Nobody can deny it. That mental attitude, as you say, is no doubt connected, in an underground fashion, to Judeo-Christian religion and the total power over nature man has given man, using God as intermediary. In this enterprise of domination, which functioned wonderfully well until the recent perils of contamination, technology is the matchless weapon.

For dominating nature and for dominating other people.

That's clear. And technology is incomparable quite simply because it gets immediate results. It's not like prayer! [laughs] If prayer gets results, most of the time they're invisible. You can always wait! [pause]

People are drawn by immediate results. What could be more normal? Why deprive them of it? Even sincere practitioners of Buddhism have cameras and watches. I myself have one right here.

On the other hand, if an individual has a sufficient spiritual base, he won't let himself be overwhelmed by the lure of technology and by the madness of possession. He or she will know to find the right balance, without asking for too much, and how to say: I have a camera, that's enough, I don't want another. The constant danger is to open the door to greed, one of our of most relentless enemies. It's here that the real work of the mind is put into practice.

That spiritual base you talk about is not, as Descartes said, the most widely distributed commodity in the world.

Not by a long shot. But we are working for a better distribution. We work at it every day, at this very moment. Because those who lack this balance, which is born of reflection, of a tranquil working of the mind, are the perfect slaves of technology and greed.

They even get to the point of believing that the real work of the mind is to produce mechanical objects. They see in them the triumph of thought, our loveliest work. They hand out diplomas to themselves and medals at contests; they collect their benefits, they're satisfied.

As you say, there's nothing wrong with technology in itself, nor is there with progress in either a material or intellectual sense. But can the human mind adapt to that technology without becoming intoxicated by it?

All the more reason for insisting. A balance is indispensable. But that balance must not be sought by forcibly lowering the level of technological realization. That would be absurd and probably unfeasible. It has to be sought for by raising the level of mind.

One thing which strikes me is that the countries that are highly developed technologically, like yours, often have to confront other absences, a sort of void that people often talk to me about: a vacuum of the mind, of spiritual life.

Western brains work, they work a great deal, but always in the direction of efficiency. In that way the mind puts itself at the service of the result. Like all servants, it renounces its independence. I'm talking about another form of spiritual life, more detached and deeper, free from the obsession of a goal to be reached. In a way, the universal invasion of technology, everywhere it goes, lessens the life of the mind.

So the life of the mind would have to be restored?

Yes. And it's urgent. Even from a simply egotistical point of view: we need additional mind more than we need additional technology. The appetite for the concrete is part of human nature and it's normal. We want to see, we want to touch, we want to get. From that standpoint, with all that it has achieved, the twentieth century has probably surpassed our most ancient dreams. Men have created objects that surprised them. All the areas of desire have been explored and often satisfied.

At least in theory, these objects still have to be acquired.

Of course. And it must be added that nothing is ever established for good, nothing is stable. Buddhism is very useful on this score. It helps us to prepare ourselves for the crumbling of empires, of received ideas. Also for the overthrow of our desires.

At the end of the '60s we thought that physical love had been miraculously freed from the old restraints. Medicine made it possible to fight venereal disease and at the same time to eliminate the fear of pregnancy. Then AIDS came along. Death by sex has come back, more terrifying than ever.

There is a drunkenness from the power that we give ourselves over things. That drunkenness leads us to stop controlling our appetites. We want more, and still more.

Instead of quelling the fire, we reignite it. Instead of seeking inner disarmament, the only kind that counts, we perfect ourselves, we multiply our tools of conquest. And we even forget to check whether the fulfillment of our desire is really the one we had wished for.

Our world is increasingly uniform in appearance, and yet it's harder, harder than ever perhaps, to find something universal in it. . .

Like Buddhism!

I know it's a difficult question, but what can we expect from Asia now and in the future? Looking at the West, Christianity is now nothing but a surface, a kind of obligation or social decoration.

That's part of the problem. Religion doesn't play its role anymore.

Assuming it ever did. All its history shows how it has been more preoccupied with worldly pursuits, even the exercise of power, than with the profoundly spiritual domain.

The domain people call 'spiritual' is often satisfied with the recitation of the Scriptures and commentary on them, whatever the tradition may be, as if all the truth of the mind, given two thousand years ago, could just be constantly repeated, and that would be enough.

Whereas the very nature of the mind seems to be a perpetual self-questioning.

In any case, it has the power to do this.

I often want something that I can no longer find at home, in our religions, our traditions, and our texts. When I read Thomas Aquinas or Augustine, they never talk to me about myself. The supposed divine element crushes every page. It's impossible for me to adhere to our credo. I can't believe, even in some allegorical sense, that God created heaven and earth, then the light, then day and night, the stars, etcetera . . .

I'm left wondering. So what were the heavens without the stars? What was the light without day? I know the millions of questions raised by these mythic texts that have long been considered – and still are, by some – to be historical. But that doesn't interest me. I don't see anything in that laborious decoding process that strikes me as a worthwhile pursuit. Besides, isn't it a serious mistake to confuse spiritual life with religious life?

They are separate. There's no doubt about that. I've often had occasion to say it. Our Scriptures affirm that the moon is a hundred miles above the earth, and that the center of the earth is Mount Meru. If that mountain exists, we should have found it a long time ago, or at least we should have discovered some signs of its existence. Since that isn't the case, we have to distance ourselves from the literal sense of the Scriptures.

And if some refuse to do this?

That's their business. It's useless to waste our time arguing with them.

Faith itself, or belief, the Dalai Lama tells me, in the sense that you give these words, has a limited place in Buddhism. The founder himself has unambiguously sent us back to our personal verification, and his teaching always invites us to 'come see'. Far from blindfolding our eyes by ordering us to believe, he takes pains to remove every obscurity, to sharpen and prolong our attention. Faith doesn't begin until reason stops.

Unlike practically all of the monotheistic religions, which are built on an unreasoning or 'blind' faith, Buddhism insists on phenomena that we can see, touch, and understand. The Sanskrit word *sraddha*, which we generally translate as 'belief', also means 'confidence born of conviction'. Responding one day to a young disciple who asked him about the ancient established truth, transmitted by the brahmans from generation to generation, Sakyamuni made him admit that none of these brahmans had personally seen and touched the truth. They were all content to repeat it like a lesson learned by rote. The Buddha compared those generations of brahmans to a long line of blind men: each one was clutching the one in front of him, and no one saw anything.

Of course, one has to introduce some nuances into this picture. So much 'confidence' has been built up and perpetuated with regard to the words of the Awakened One, that we might well say that for Buddhists the truth of those words is quite simply the object of belief, at least in popular devotion. Anyway, Buddhism has analyzed and explicated the notion of faith, as it does for all our ideas. But at a higher level, where speculation, the methodical doubt, and the most pointed oratorical jousting remain the order of the day, the principle of authority is gradually fading away. All throughout our conversations, the Dalai Lama never once produced an affirmation that could be called dogmatic. He never told me, 'That's how it is because that's how it is', or 'Because the Buddha said so', or 'Because it can be found in (this or that) text'. Never, except perhaps on one point, which is concerned with reincarnation. We shall return to that.

4

It's from within that I Resemble You

In the third issue of the review *La Révolution surréaliste*, for April 1925, we find this collective text entitled *Address to the Dalai Lama*:

> We are your most faithful servants, O Great Lama, give us your wisdom, send it our way, in a language that our contaminated European minds can understand. And if necessary, change our Mind, make us a mind entirely turned toward the perfect summits where the Mind of Man no longer suffers.
>
> Make us a mind without habits, a mind truly frozen in Mind, or a mind with purer habits, your habits, if they are good for freedom.
>
> We are surrounded by rough popes, by littérateurs, by critics, by dogs; our Mind is among the dogs, who think immediately with the earth, who think incorrigibly in the present.
>
> Teach us, Lama, the material levitation of bodies and how we may no longer be held down by the earth. For you well know to what transparent liberation of souls, to what freedom of the

Mind in the Mind, o acceptable Pope, o Pope in the veritable mind, we are alluding.

It is with the inner eye that I look upon you, o Pope, at the inner summit. It is from within that I resemble you, myself, thrust, idea, lip, levitation, dream, cry, renunciation of the idea, suspended between all the forms and no longer hoping for anything but the wind.

This text, written by several young surrealist artists, clearly echoes the feeling which even today can be so fascinating about this kind of Buddhism; it's not a change of beliefs, but a real metamorphosis of the mind. The open letter to the Dalai Lama was a cry from the surrealist heart: 'It is from within that I resemble you', is in that sense its most distinctive phrase.

If we have a hard time seeing these surrealists spinning prayer wheels, we *can* by contrast imagine them searching for 'purer habits' and an ever higher quality of mind leading them 'to the inner summit'. *That* is the domain from where Buddhism never ceases to launch its appeal.

This point you raised about spiritual and religious life is extremely important. We've got to go back to it. Many think these two activities are really just one. Religious leaders, here and there, loudly proclaim that they own the territory of the spirit, that it's their fief. By the same token, to hear them talk, anyone who rejects religion is ipso facto rejecting all spiritual experience.

Which is perfectly excessive. Why should spiritual life necessarily be linked to some supernatural belief? We could almost say the opposite, that faith means abandoning the spirit or the mind.

Yes, you could say that. But I'm not looking to turn anyone away from their faith, if they practice it with tolerance. Still, look where the confusion between religious and spiritual can lead: let's imagine a man who talks about the notion of goodwill or forgiveness, or again of compassion, the attitude that, as you know, is one of the foundations of Buddhism. Another man who has no religious concerns, listens to the first man, and says with a shrug of his shoulders: 'All that is religion, it doesn't interest me.'

He's absolutely wrong. He has fallen into a crude vocabulary trap! The words 'compassion' or 'charity' have blinded him.

Now this is about human, purely human, qualities. We don't need a divine revelation to get them or discover them. Of course, in theory all religions recommend compassion, and tolerance too, generosity, the taste for knowledge, all the good human qualities.

But they can't corner the market on them.

In no way. That's an illegitimate attitude. Look at the animals; one could say that they manifest a certain mutual aid, a certain tolerance, and even that they show compassion for one another. But it's clear that in this area human feelings seem more profound and stubborn. When humans reach the point of the highest quality, they can also show disinterest, which seems to me much rarer, if not totally absent, among the animals. On that specifically human base we have gradually built up certain concepts, which vary from one culture to another, such as the creator god, heaven, hell, *nirvana*, or *moksha*, which is liberation from our fetters, and still others. These concepts can be proclaimed as universal, valid for all human beings, without distinction of race, tradition, or character.

Proclaimed, and often imposed by force.

Yes, unfortunately. But one can also say that, as is the case with Buddhism, that these notions don't have to be strictly respected except by practitioners. You can propose them to others without imposing them. Even if we consider [such notions] universal, we respect in other people all the particular features that forbid [those people] to accept them. Everyone has to be free to accept or refuse this or that belief or concept

People remain free to adhere to what they want?

Of course.

For a long time the West has been wondering about that supposed freedom. Aren't we ruled by the community where we are born, by the beliefs that surround us, by our childhood, by all the elements that makes us up?

That's certain. And that's why the task is so difficult. But I can say that at a certain level of reflection we always have a choice. We can get that freedom, and detach ourselves from everything that blocks us. And we must do this. I once said that it seems to me that God has fallen asleep somewhere. I was joking, as you might imagine, since we make no allowance for a creator god. But it is true that if God has fallen asleep, then it's our job to wake Him up.

One can't blame all our troubles on God.

Nor on destiny, nor on *karma*, which is our law of the chain of causes, of deeds, and effects. All that comes from a rather cowardly attitude. If it is true – as I believe – that the diversity of religious attitudes is a faithful reflection of human diversity, then we mustn't look for our unity in some belief.

But in action instead?

In responsible and thoughtful action. In a domain like that of the environment, which we've talked a lot about, it seems to me that out of simple common sense we all ought to agree, like children when the life of their mother is at stake.

Can we also survive without religion?

Of course we can. Figure it out: there are more than 5 billion of us on the planet. Three billion have no sort of religion. Of the 2 billion who call themselves religious, I would say that only a billion of the followers of this or that religion are sincere believers. One billion in five, that means a minority. Evidently we have to work today for the other 4 billion.

Everything starts with us, with each one of us. The indispensable qualities are peace of mind and compassion. Without them it's useless even to try. Those qualities are indispensable; they are also inevitable. I've told you: we will surely find them in ourselves, if we take the trouble to search for them. We can reject every form of religion but we can't reject and cast off compassion and peace of mind.

Still, some individuals seem to get there rather easily.

Of course, and for a number of reasons, one of which is ignorance. I never talk about the totality of human beings. I know perfectly well that they present differences which sometimes go to extreme distortions. I talk about men and women of goodwill, who have the desire to do something with their lives.

Clinging to an unknowable and unattainable God – isn't that dodging the responsibility of which you speak?

In some cases, perhaps. But not necessarily. The idea of God can also lead to beautiful acts of compassion.

And in prohibitions, exclusions, murders.

That's the danger of any faith.

It can lead to the inner obligation of making others share, by all means, what one takes to be an eternal truth, and which is never anything but relative . . .

Like all truths!

Perhaps there is a god, but we mustn't expect anything from him.

In other words, whether God exists or not, in any event He doesn't exist?

Yes – but maybe He's the one who brought us together here?

It's customary to say that Buddhism was born and developed in India, two centuries after the death of Buddha, and especially during the reign of King Asoka (273–232 B.C.), as a reaction against Brahmanism, the traditional religion about which we know little. The parallel history of these two traditions ended later with the progressive weakening and quasi-disappearance of Buddhism in India and its expansion through Asia. That history is made up not just of conflict but of reciprocal influences and exchanges.

Without getting into a comparative analysis, which would take several volumes, it's worthwhile to stress a few differences. Brahmanism, also called Hinduism, admits a multitude of mythological gods and tales. Depending on the traditions, the creation of the world is recounted in various ways. Without having the divine omnipotence of the monotheistic religions, the Indian gods – who are subject to the great cycles of time, the *yugas* – can interfere in human affairs; and they are sometimes considered mortal. Today the 36,000 divinities of the Indian pantheon, quite apart from the many popular cults, are often used as a sort of immense vocabulary to help people talk about the mystery of the world.

Human life confronts four fundamental notions or activities, which are called in Sanskrit *dharma, artha, kama,* and *moksha*.

Dharma is the great law of the universe, the order to which we must submit. The peculiar feature of Hindu tradition is its affirmation that this universal law can also be found in each one of us, that we all have an individual dharma that we must follow with diligence. We have to know who we are and remain faithful to what we are. If our particular dharmas are respected, the universal *Dharma* will be preserved. Thus Hinduism introduces a sort of solidarity between the human being and the cosmos. Asked about the reasons that drove him to compose the great epic of the *Mahabharata*, Vyasa answered, 'To inscribe the *Dharma* in the heart of men.'

This peculiarly Indian notion has been kept by Buddhism. The Buddhist dharma remains the totality of phenomena subject to law. But the word has taken on a more precise sense of doctrine, teaching of the Buddha, prescribed duties. Even if the cosmological aspect has become somewhat attenuated, in favour of a more human observance, the Dharma remains the guide for every life, the indispensable source of knowledge.

The second notion is *artha*, a word that generally means 'the good things of the earth'. Contrary to doctrines that insist on renunciation, Hinduism tends to say that the good things of this world have been given to us to be enjoyed, and that renunciation is nothing if we don't know what we are renouncing. Thus Hinduism advises us not to leave society to become wandering ascetics, or *sadhus*, before getting to know our children's children. In Buddhism it happens that children are selected from their earliest years and consecrated to a monastic life (which they can leave without difficulty).

The third fundamental notion is *kama*, which is love, the mover of the worlds, and more particularly sexual love. The god Kama is a sort of Cupid, often depicted with a bow and wings, shooting flowered arrows. It's the action of *kama* that most often determines the cycle of rebirths, *samsara*. It is he 'who intoxicates', 'who agitates the mind', 'the invisible conqueror'. In Hinduism this force can extend to the movement of the universe. In general Buddhism remains more cautious on the universe. In general Buddhism remains more cautious on this point – except in Tantric tradition.

Finally the fourth notion is *moksha*, which is liberation the ultimate deliverance from the cycle of rebirths, which is located in the highest degree of consciousness. In Hinduism this deliverance leads to fusion with Brahma, the universal being. In Buddhism, where the same word is used, it prefigures *nirvana*. On the highest conceivable level of consciousness, where the mind becomes 'subtle', it can reach awakening, the Buddha-state.

Among the perfect beings, who have a lively aspiration for that awakening and who have every possibility of getting there, the Buddhist tradition called the Grand Vehicle or Mahayana (which interests us here, because Tibetan Buddhism invokes it) gives a major role to the *bodhisattvas*. These beings, who are in a way intermediaries between us and the Buddha-state, and who could lay claim to the eternal blessedness of *nirvana*, prefer to renounce it for the sake of remaining behind to help us. As long a human suffering persists, we can count on them. Thus they act out of pure compassion for us.

Before his incarnation in the person of Prince Siddhartha, the Buddha, in the course of his prior existence, was the *bodhisattva* par excellence. A great many others came after him. The most venerated of them, the man who is the very essence of compassion (to the point that the other *bodhisattvas* are sometimes considered his derivatives and manifestations) was called Avalokiteshvara. He was 'the one who gives the thirsty to drink', the 'brilliant lord who looks down', 'he who bears the lotus', the most popular of intercessors. There are many different representations of him, and he can take on a great number of aspects. At this moment nobody at Dharamsala has any doubt that he has taken the form of the man who sits beside me, talks to me, looks at me, and sometimes clasps my hands.

Among the various effigies to be seen in the room where we find ourselves, some are ancient, saved from Tibet at the moment when the Dalai Lama went off into exile in 1959; others have been made right here. These gilded presences are reassuring, surrounded by little bouquets of artificial flowers. Among them, rather strangely, I find no image of Avalokiteshvara. It's true that he's alive, right here.

If we set aside the unverifiable idea of a god who is the creator and supreme judge, we come to the notion of what might be called 'a human religion' (or 'humanistic religion'), that is to say, born of human reflection to meet a human need. In that sense the notion of the *bodhisattva* is perhaps more scientific than all the theological reflections.

The lived notion of the *bodhisattva* is no doubt one of the elements that nowadays increasingly attracts curious minds to Buddhism. I really believe that Buddhism is more profound and more sophisticated than other religions or schools of thought.

Which doesn't mean that Buddhism is superior or even better. Nor, above all, that it's applicable to everyone. For certain believers, the creator god is a more powerful concept, perhaps even more accessible, better adapted to certain peoples, to certain cultures.

This is because of the very force of habit, of tradition. It's absurd to think that in a single movement an entire tradition is going to collapse, that all men and women, as if by a miracle, are suddenly going to cherish the same hopes, rely on the same faith, the same thought. When we meet a very different belief, or even an opposite one, but deeply and sincerely established, we have to respect it.

It's the same for food. You can't say that such and such a food is good for everyone. That depends on the climate, on eating habits, the altitude, and on how old you are, perhaps. It depends on a great variety of circumstances.

It's the same for the notion of Buddhism. I believe deeply that it's more thoughtful and better adapted to today's world than many other religious concepts are. I have had many visitors talk to me about it. They feel very close to the force of compassion that we find at the most constant level of our inconstant nature and that the *bodhisattva* in some way personifies. Among those visitors I often meet scientists. But this interest that people have doesn't give us any right to judge others by our particularism. We don't own the universal truth, we can offer only the results of a very long reflection, which is ours.

So the notion of the bodhisattva *would be relative, too?*

Of course. We have no right to apply it in general, to make it into a universal dogma. When I present a teaching, I always take a lot of precautions. I say, 'Pay close attention, don't make crucial decisions lightly. It's a major break with the past to change your religion, your way of life or thought. Think about it a good long time.'

This rather exceptional attitude relies once again on an episode drawn from the life of Sakyamuni. When the Buddha was engaged in preaching, the founder of Jainism, Mahavira, was also preaching in the north of India. Mahavira was a considerable personage and no doubt older than Sakyamuni.

It happened that Mahavira, having heard talk about the teaching of the newcomer, which differed from his, dispatched one of his disciples, a rich layman named Upali, to meet Sakyamuni and to challenge him to a public disputation on the idea of *karma*. In the course of that disputation Upali was rather quickly convinced by the arguments of Sakyamuni. This prompted him to ask the Buddha to accept him as a lay disciple.

Sakyamuni replied that his decision was too hasty. He advised him to reflect deeply on it. When Upali pressed him again, the Buddha refused to keep with him and sent him back to his old master, telling him to respect and support him.

Buddhism never stops reminding us that the truth has no label. The example comes from way back, from the Enlightened One himself, who turned down every hasty form or recruitment, and also from King Asoka. He was the first sovereign of India to convert to Buddhism, but despite that the king continued to manifest goodwill toward other beliefs.

When, in the wake of Constantine, the Roman emperors converted to Christianity, their attitude toward the pagans and Jews was totally different. Like some of their predecessors they took the path of persecution.

The affirmations by Buddhists today don't mean that the history of Buddhism was exempt from all violence. China in particular experienced some harsh confrontations in the Middle Ages. Despite the recognized tolerance of the Tang sovereigns, some of them, such as the Empress Wu Hou (625–705), didn't hesitate to use Buddhism for brutal political purposes.

That's how humans are, the Dalai Lama would say. Hence, in spite of the official tolerance, there has to be an unyielding vigilance – mainly toward ourselves.

Where does intolerance come from? From within or without? From a sincere attachment to a conviction, or from a taste for pomp and circumstance, for power, for the incense that arises from large prostrate crowds?

How are we to get rid of these temptations, how – to borrow the words of the surrealists – can we 'make ourselves a mind without habits', how 'be held no longer by the earth'?

5

Toward a Science of the Mind

Dealing with Hindu and Buddhist ideas isn't easy, not just because of the terms themselves, which are difficult to transcribe, but also because of our wish to give them a precise meaning in other languages, to find equivalents in other systems of thought. Thus the word *Dharma* or *bodhisattva* can't be translated into French or English. The roots of these words have no associations for us. The meaning we give them is dry, disembodied, colourless. If we keep them in the original language, Sanskirt or Pali, we need a lot of patience before we can really appreciate and feel them. Even an apparently universal notion such as compassion takes on a peculiar consistency in Buddhism. Far from looking like a natural feeling, made up of gentleness and amiability, sentimental, at bottom a little banal and even a bit kitschy (for many readers in a hurry Buddhism can be summed up in a single phrase: 'It's better to be nice than nasty'), compassion is the object of careful study. To borrow an expression from Sogyal Rinpoche, there is 'a logic of compassion', whose stages, operations, and results (in others but also in ourselves) can be studied in a quasi-scientific fashion.

When we came to speak about the concept of the *bodhisattva*, the Dalai Lama began to worry about the increasing difficulty with vocabulary. I tried to reassure him and pressed him not to be deterred from using what might seem difficult or even inaccessible in a simple book. We discussed the similar problems faced by scientists when they want to address a wide audience. I spoke to him about a book I wrote with two astro-physicists, Jean Audouze and Michel Cassé, where the same problems were presented. How, for example, can we imagine an atom, and the particles in that atom?

I tell him about an image I got from those two experts. Take an orange, enlarge it to the size of the earth. Then fill that gigantic orange with cherries: this will give you roughly the number of atoms in one orange. It's a rather large number around 10^{20}.

That's only a gimmick to try to get the mind used to imagining the unimaginable, in this case, the infinitely small. But then it shows us that at the end of its analysis the most up-to-date science, like Buddhism, finds the void.

This scientific discussion continues with a discussion of neutrinos. Astrophysics teachers us that at every moment a continuous current of billions of ultra-fine particles – neutrinos – is passing through us. Coming from the sun and other stars, they pass through our flesh and through our planet with utter indifference without being slowed in the least. Interestingly enough, though, neutrinos are something unfamiliar to the Dalai Lama; he has real interest in the concept and takes extra time in our conversation to ensure he understands it.

We talk for a moment about this bit of common ground, about this enigmatic void that we are to our own eyes, about impermanence too, which seems to sweep away everything, even those streams of unconquerable particles that travel effortlessly through the universe. I think of one of the most beautiful texts of Japanese Buddhism, the *Kegonkyo*, a sutra of the Kegon teaching: 'Illumined with his own light, the Buddha brightens all the universes. His pure look knows all things and penetrates everywhere. He reveals himself in the infinite, and he *is* the infinite. . .'

A little farther on in the same text, it is said that he 'resides at the center of the most minuscule atom.' Here an ancient and lasting intuition speaks intimately to us. At first, contrary to the restrained conceptions of the West, and particularly of Aristotle, who conditioned our view of the cosmos at least until the time of Galileo, the East has always sensed the universe as unlimited, expanding everywhere. The worlds it contains are countless. Buddhism describes it as a long series of huge rings threaded on an invisible axis, the famous Mount Meru. Hinduism calls that axis 'Dharma', and sees it as maintained by Vishnu. Here, too, the universe, far from limiting itself to the vault of the heavens, is of spectacular dimensions, which the poets exhaust themselves describing. Indra, the king of the gods, lives in a special capital, Amaravati, which is always moving in space.

Second, according to the oldest Buddhist texts, the matter of the world is made up of very fine particles, or *anu*, a word generally translated as 'atoms'. These particles have substance and are indivisible. Some schools go so far as to say that these atoms don't touch and don't interrelate or form wholes except by the force of the element of wind. Thus the wind assures the cohesion of the aggregates of particles, which are generally translated as 'molecules'. These molecules, perpetually unstable (like all composite bodies) contain all the elementary substances and all the qualities that derive from them (taste, odour, appearance, tangible consistency, sound). Furthermore, inside these molecules and groups of molecules all the elements coexist: water contains fire and earth, otherwise that water could neither heat up nor freeze.

Finally (I am quoting verbatim): 'Thus the bodies that it [the molecule] has are perceptible, and perception of them takes place when the objective molecules are joined by similar molecules located in the sense organs, for example on the pupil for sight. . . .'

That reminds me of a phrase of Michel Cassé, where he speaks of the sun, the fashioner of our eye: 'The atom of the sun speaks the language of light to the atom of the eye.'

In the middle of one of our conversations, it suddenly occurred to me to ask, 'Couldn't Buddhism be described as a sort of science? A science of the mind?' The Dalai Lama answered at once, 'That's exactly it!' When I then asked him to tell me about the mind, he burst out laughing. Grabbing the sleeve of my sweater, he said, 'For that you'd have to change clothes, put on a red robe, and do nothing but study for twelve years!'

The science of the mind, of the mind's functioning, is an ancient and remarkably refined activity in the history of Buddhism. Since nothing can be seen or conceived without the mind, since, according to certain schools, all the things in the universe can be manifestations of mind, this science is necessary. It is at the heart of our study.

Given that objects have only a relative or conventional existence, and that it's impossible to consider them in themselves, as independent and stable entities, the approach to these objects by our senses is delicate, subject to a thousand errors and dogged by confusion. One of the founders of Mahayana, Nāgārjuna – whom the Dalai Lama often quotes as one of his favorite masters – wrote at the beginning of the third century:

The farther we are away form the world,
The realer it seems to us;
The closer we get to it, the less visible it becomes
And, like a mirage, becomes without a sign.

In this text we rediscover both the imperious necessity of 'seeing' and the inevitable confusion brought on by every attempt to 'see up close'. Long before this the Buddha had already affirmed: 'Form is like a magical illusion, and sensations, perceptions, mental formations, and consciousness are magical illusion too.'

It seems to me that this difficulty of attaining the real is at the core of the Buddhist study of mind.

Yes, without a doubt. Hence there are many precautions to be taken, and divisions and subdivisions in the way we approach the subject. For example, with regard to direct perceptions (which aren't the only kind), all the Buddhist traditions distinguish three types: sensory, mental, and yogic. The last kind can be reached only through meditation.

But aren't these three types of perception divided into several categories?

Yes, into a number of levels, which in their turn have to be connected with the six kinds of consciousness and fifty-one mental factors, which are present only on occasion. You see why if you want to know everything, you'll have to shave your head!

Apply a little simple arithmetic, and the number of possible combinations of perceptual operations very quickly becomes enormous. Yet each one of these operations has been minutely described and analyzed – and often criticized or doubted – by centuries of study. It's the same for the other operations of the mind such as cognition, conceptual thought, or memory. The list seems to be so incredibly long that no individual today could master all of that science. No mind can grasp all that is in the mind.

This fascination that the human mind feels concerning itself is bound up with another feeling, which is easier to express, and tirelessly repeated: the body is condemned to decrepitude, and we can't do anything about it. Buddhist authors almost seem to enjoy dwelling on the loss of our hair, the weakening of our vision, the growing heaviness of our limbs. By contrast, if our body inevitably declines, we can constantly beautify our mind, up until our last hour. It has even been said that at the moment of death, if we are well prepared, we can finally receive the essential revelations.

There is another factor reinforcing the confusion here: our mind is by nature undisciplined. In the wonderful text of the *Bhagvad-Gita* the hero Arjuna, suddenly struck by the incapacity to fight, says to Krishna, his charioteer and friend: 'The mind is capricious and unstable, it is fleeting and feverish, turbulent and tenacious. Overcoming it seems to me harder than mastering the wind. How to decide? How to choose?'

Krishna himself realizes that the mind is 'mysterious and incomprehensible', undoubtedly 'greater than the senses'. To learn the secret functioning of the mind is to advance through the thick forest of illusion. It is at the same time to grasp the whole course of the world.

This apprehension of the mind as a disordered whirlwind has been described many times in Buddhism, both directly and metaphorically. 'The mind is produced and dispersed in a perpetual process of change,' Sakyamuni said. 'Just as an ape cavorting in the forest seizes one branch, then lets go of it to seize another, and then still others, so what you call mind, thought, knowledge, is ceaselessly formed and dissolved.'

From a lack of discipline, the mind in its activity is irresistibly drawn by the forms of illusion. It is continuously deceived about the reality of the world. The image of the ape returns again and again: our mind is also an ape locked up in an empty house, into which several openings have been cut. These openings are our sense organs. The ape casts a glance through the window, perceives a rectangular slice of the outside world, moves on immediately to another window, without reflection, without any effort at criticism or synthesis. This brings about a fragmentary, mutilated, necessarily false perception, which leads to actions that are rapid, brutal, and always baneful.

As for the mind itself, it has no particular characteristics. Apart from the aberrant influence of the senses, it is indifferent as a mirror reflecting whatever is placed in front of it. An eleventh-century Indian master put it this way: 'The luminous mind has neither colour nor form. It isn't dark or clear, neither bad nor good.' It's useless to attribute any original and inseparable qualities to it. It is beyond qualifying. By its very function, it is perhaps the only real creator. Thus it constitutes an obligatory passage. It's impossible to dissipate illusion without dealing with the mind. As another great master, Shantideva (seventh century) said: 'If one has not first of all apprehended the phenomenon constructed by the mind, its nonexistence cannot be established.'

Finally the phenomena constructed by the mind are all the more difficult to discern because it has a mysterious region that we now call the unconscious. This surprising discovery was made by the Buddha, at the very beginning. He called this impenetrable territory *amushaya*. In the same way, he said, that physiological processes such as digestion are carried out within our body but unbeknownst to us, so our thought can bury in itself preoccupations and dangerous attachments. These are all the more dangerous because we think they have been wiped out, but they have only been hidden away and disguised even from ourselves. Even if we offer, on the surface, some appearance of peace, we still harbour a volcano inside ourselves.

Sakyamuni supplies a brief definition of *amushaya* to which we can add nothing: 'the underground habit of dependence and aversion.'

Don't worry, we can talk about the mind. Often enough I find myself bringing up the subject with scientists, neurologists, psychiatrists. In the last few years I've taken part in five or six such meetings.

How did it go?

In the beginning they hesitate a little. I sense that they're reticent. Evidently they're afraid I'll be content to hand out a list of dogmatic statements. On the second or third day, as the discussions continue, bit by bit their reticence lessens, and sometimes disappears altogether. Far from seeing Buddhism as a rigid religion, some of them are willing to realize that it's a matter, as you say, of science. And like all sciences this science, extremely complex as it is, is based on experience.

Which scientists struck you as the most interested?

The psychologists, the neurologists, all those who study the brain, and also the physicists and astrophysicists, the ones who work on the stuff of the universe, on the elementary particles.

Did you get into quantum mechanics?

Yes, as best I could.

You know that on the level of the infinitely small the mind reaches a territory of uncertainty?

I was told that. It didn't really surprise me.

This uncertainty, posited by Heisenberg and Niels Bohr, has defied investigation for more than fifty years. In the physics of infinitely small particles, it's impossible to know both the position of an electron and its velocity. The mind has to choose. That categorical limit on knowledge, which has been confirmed by other observations, seems to pose a rather radical challenge to the usual relations between the mind and reality.

Unlike the East, the West has never radically doubted the existence of reality. According to our classical tradition, God has put the laws into nature; and our task, as Descartes says, is to discover them. This is an attitude that the West has been questioning only since the beginning of the twentieth century, since relativity and quantum mechanics, though not without being disconcerted and amazed. Without going so far as radically to doubt reality, and without renouncing the establishment of laws (even if in some areas they are accompanied by a fringe of incertitude), contemporary researchers are introducing into their work a new dimension, which is precisely the relationship to mind. The observer, by his or her very presence, by his or her faintest intervention, modifies the object observed. All research today has to take this into account. The relation becomes more important than the object.

In this domain, even though it takes other paths, Eastern thought has gone before us. I tell the Dalai Lama that one day, while we were working together, I called astrophysicist Michel Cassé to read to him this phrase: 'Everything that exists, mobile or immobile, arises from the union of the field and the knower of the field.'

Cassé immediately replied: 'But that's one of the most beautiful definitions of quantum mechanics I ever heard.'

Then I informed him that I had just read a phrase of Krishna's in the *Bhagavad-Gita*, a phrase often badly mistranslated in the nineteenth century (as 'union of matter and mind', for example, whereas the two Sanskrit words are almost the same: *kshetra*, which literally means 'field', and *kshetrajna*, 'the one who knows the field'), until the appearance of quantum mechanics finally allowed a correct interpretation.

The phrase in no way permits us to say that Krishna, or the authors of the poem, knew about Heisenberg's principle and the secrets of particle physics. That would be a pure fantasy. But there's no dodging the fact that an ancient intuition, expressed quite often in Indian and Tibetan tradition, affirms the inseparability of our mind, our senses, and things. On that point Buddhism is especially peremptory.

The Dalai Lama has visited the CERN (European Center for Nuclear Research), he has taken part in scientific discussions at Harvard as well as in Grenoble. These parallels are nothing alien to him. He accepts them with no great surprise, as if our science were rediscovering an ancient path – which we must be careful to avoid interpreting as a meeting of technologies and research findings. The world of the ancient East never had some kind of technical secrets that we somehow lost. Quite simply, in this essential sphere, which brings into play the mind and the object that the mind is seeking (which might be itself), the traditions we mentioned have refused to separate one from the other. Today, thanks to the simple passage of time, which shapes our ideas as well, East and West are coming to understand one another, sometimes even to merge into one another.

The fact remains that the Dalai Lama, a convinced adept of the middle way, keeps telling us to distrust extreme positions. He wonders if Western thought, so greedy for certitude, balanced between classical dualism and contemporary confusion, doesn't tend to neglect 'the gray zone,' that middle territory where the mind is part of things.

I believe deeply that we must find, all of us together, a new spirituality.

Which wouldn't be 'religious'?

Certainly not. This new concept ought to be elaborated alongside the religions, in such a way that all people of goodwill could adhere to it.

Even if they have no religion, or are against religion?

Absolutely. We need a new concept, a lay spirituality. We ought to promote this concept, with the help of scientists. It could lead us to set up what we are all looking for, *a secular morality*. I believe in it deeply. And I think we need it so the world can have a better future.

Every day I experience the benefits of peace of mind. It's very good for the body. As you might imagine, I am a rather busy man. I take many responsibilities upon myself, activities, trips, speeches. All that no doubt is a very heavy burden, and still I have the blood pressure of a baby.

Last year in Washington, at the Walter Reed Army Hospital, they took my blood pressure. And the doctor said, 'Wow, I wish mine was the same!'

What's good for me is good for other people. I have no doubt on that score. Good food, a struggle against every excessive desire, daily meditation, all that can lead to peace of mind, and peace of mind is good for the body. Despite all the difficulties of life, of which I've had my share, we can all feel that effect.

And the path is still compassion?

Exactly. Compassion. The logical feeling that we find in ourselves if we search deeply enough and that has to be exercised toward all other living creatures. Even if sometimes that seems hard. Thus, at this moment I'm striving to feel compasison for those who are called my enemies, for the Chinese who have invaded Tibet. The action they have committed, and that they continue to commit, contribute to their bad *karma*, for which one day or another they will be punished.

Karma, an idea inherited from Hinduism, but broadly developed in Buddhism, is a 'law of acts'. All the things that we can do and all the thoughts that we can think (Buddhism clings methodically to the principle that there is no fact without a cause and no cause without an effect) constitute a sort of energy, or force, whose effects will be felt one day, in this life or in another. That force, for each consciousness, determines the quality of its future reincarnations. Thus bad or negative *karma* pushes you farther away from the final realization, the longed-for escape from the cycle of rebirths, or *samsara*.

Some writers, such as Jorge Luis Borges, who saw in *karma* an 'inconceivable structure', have wondered what authority was the source of this 'law of acts', since no divine creator watches over the observance of the laws that he supposedly traced out. In other words, who has established *karma?* Who guarantees it functioning? In what form does that force present itself, since in Buddhism there is no particular soul that could transmigrate from one body to another? The answers vary according to the school.

In our discussion, the Dalai Lama insists on compassion, which returns like a leitmotif in his conversations. This insistence is no doubt at the root of a certain naiveté that is sometimes attributed to his remarks in the rapid give-and-take of discussions. To say that 'we ought to feel compassion for others' could pass for a catechism banality, bathed in fine sentiments, easy to say and quite simply utopian.

This objection fails to see that the Dalai Lama's affirmation is the total opposite of a superficial, all-purpose maxim. It is in fact the result of extremely careful research. In the final analysis the compassion he speaks of is in us; it's a feeling that is peculiar to us and more powerful than our violent instincts. But many negative forces, which we constantly see manifesting themselves around us, and in ourselves as well, obscure that profound energy and stifle it in our own eyes. Hence we have to search continuously for compassion within us; we have to recognize and practice it.

If only for selfish purposes. Because the compassion that I practice does me good in return. It is the best protection, and I am the first beneificary of it. It assures me inner peace, a healthy body, happy days, a long life. Not to mention the lives to come.

Let's deal first of all with this one.

You're right. Besides, the other lives depend upon it. Well, in this life, which quickens you and me at this moment, we all want to live in a united community, to enjoy good health, a harmonious family, in short to have a happy life. . . .

And a happy death. . . .

Yes. And a happy rebirth!*

We owe a great deal to peace of mind. For us it's a matter of fact. That boils down to saying that we owe a great deal to the mind itself. The whole history of Buddhism brings us back to the mind, to our mind. A considerable amount of work has been done by the mind on the mind. And we continue to do it.

By getting to the very illusion of history?

That is true for some schools.

---

* He laughs heartily here, well aware that I have little confidence in any other birth or any other life!

But what is the exact meaning of the word 'illusion'? Can one conceive of an illusion without an illusionist?

We say that the mind deludes itself, at every moment, in the summary perception that it has of the world. And that this erroneous perception has to be corrected, unless we choose to live in error. We say that our natural agitation leads us astray, that no real relationship can be established with the world if we don't get to peace of mind.

Thus Sakyamuni was the first (with hundreds of other thinkers and meditators in his wake) to track down the very existence of the mind, with a pitiless logic (the thinker must have no compassion for his or her own thought). That is, since the external world, pierced by our senses, is devoid of any intrinsic reality, the effects that it has on our senses are equally empty and illusory. Our ideas, which in their turn are born of our sense perceptions, are therefore devoid of real meaning and truth. And finally, our voluntary decisions, which generally arise from our ideas, are thus deprived of any solid foundation.

As Maurice Percheron wrote: 'The synthesis of these diverse groups of elements (what we call consciousness) is thus a pure mirage.'

We can also borrow a celebrated phrase found in the *Immutable Sutra*: 'The phenomena of life can be compared to a dream, a fantasm, an air bubble, a shadow, a glistening dew, a flash of lightning, and they have to be looked upon in that way.'

How, then, can you quell a mirage? How act upon an entity – the mind – that would seem to be born of its own illusions and to take delight in perpetuating it?

The long history of Buddhism has been passionately taken up with this apparent paradox. First of all, it has recognized as a conspicuous fact that while the mind may not exist, the operations of the mind are nonetheless interlinked. We can't doubt them without preaching absurdity.

As for that peace of mind we find within us – the Dalai Lama likes to insist on this point – it's not a question of inventing it, but of rediscovering it and with it the path to true consciousness. As Ananda Coomaraswamy says, 'in the same way a lamp brought into a dark room lets us distinguish what was already there.' We were waiting peace, which is necessary and fertile. Sri Aurobindo defined it in his own way: 'Outside activities will then traverse the mind's calm as a flock of birds traverses a windless space.'

This peace of mind, I repeat, is a fact. There's no use denying it, presenting humans as the playthings of exclusively aggressive or possessive or dominating energies. Of course, all these dangerous tendencies do exist in us, but beneath them, deeper and more permanent, lies peace. If we use this peace as a fact, we can truly offer humanity the possibility of something better. But first of all it has to be recognized, attained, and preserved.

Despite what you see around you, and what you have lived through yourself, you continue to think that human nature is good?

I don't *think* so. It's not an opinion, it's a fact. There are many circumstances that make us unjust, ambitious, or aggressive. All around us, everything is pushing us in that direction, often out of some commercial interest: I have to possess this or that object, otherwise my life will be lamentable. To possess that object, I have to make extra money, I have to fight, I have to oppose others. Thus my aggressiveness reappears.

In business it's considered a good quality.

I know. The world is presented to us as essentially competitive, divided into 'the winners' and 'the losers', but that too is a false vision, deliberately false. It's a rapid scan of the surface, which eliminates any descent into the self, any meditation, and reflection.

So we're not the way we see ourselves? The way we imagine ourselves?

The image that we have of ourselves readily tends to be complacent. We look at ourselves with indulgence. When something unpleasant happens to us, we always have the tendency to caste the blame on others, or on fate, a demon, or a god. We shrink from descending into ourselves, as the Buddha recommended.

And if we descend into ourselves, we find that compassion you speak of?

Inevitably. You yourself have survived only because of the affection of others. And that's been true ever since the cradle, perhaps even since you were in your mother's womb, since they say that even before our birth we're sensitive to the environment and to the affection people feel of us. I'm convinced that a happy mother bears a happy child. If she's calm, if her mind is at peace, her child will be influenced by that.

And such affection is spontaneous, genuine. The mother expects nothing in return from her child. It's pure affection, noncalculating. But without it the child couldn't survive.

All our lives began with human affection as our first support. Children who grow up surrounded by that kind of affection smile more; they're friendlier and generally better balanced. For those who have been deprived of such affection, it's the other way around. They are harder, and they have more problems.

There are exceptions, as you surely know. The influence that shape our personality are many and complex. Some kinds of bad treatment may, on the contrary, toughen us.

Make us harder and more aggressive.

Not to mention heredity, which we can't control, though the biologists are working on that. Certain influences come from very, very far away. Some even say from the time before we were human.

That's possible. We have to accept, as I said, whatever science teaches us. Let's say that, in general, haste, competition, and all the things we call stress, thwarted ambition, the difficult road to success, the deceptive lure of money, that all those things are no good for our body, for our organism.

You have to understand that the affection I'm speaking of has no purpose, it's not given with the intention of getting anything back. It's not a matter of feeling. In the same way we say that real compassion is without attachment. Pay attention to this point, which goes against our habitual ways of thinking. It's not this or that particular case that stirs our pity. We don't give our compassion to such and such a person by choice. We give it spontaneously, entirely, without hoping for anything in exchange. And we give it universally.*

* The detachment in action was already taught by Hinduism. In the *Bhagavad-Gita* Krishna teaches Arjuna that one must act without being preoccupied with the 'fruit of the acts', the results, the profit, material or moral. If such true detachment is reached, it allows action that is true and, for

What's to be said about love and sexual desire?

Sexual desire, by definition, wants something, which is the satisfaction of desire by the possession of the other. To a large extent this is a mental projection, provoked by a certain emotion. We imagine the other in our possession. At the moment of desire everything seems agreeable and desirable. One sees no obstacle to it, no reason for restraint. The object desired seems to have no defects, to be worthy of all praise.

But then everything changes with possession?

To be sure. Once the desire disappears – whether it considers itself satisfied, or time passes and weakens it – we no longer look at the other in the same way. The appearances of the once desirable object change and sometimes rapidly, suddenly. Some people admit they are stunned by this. The emotion they started out from is dissipated, giving way to a reciprocal misunderstanding. Each one discovers the true nature of the other, which up till then had been hidden by his or her desire. That's why there are so many broken marriages, quarrels, lawsuits, hatreds.[†]

---

that very reason, irreproachable. Even the desire for victory in a battle has to be rejected, like all desire. This rejection also concerns the feeling that I might have about my own worth. I must not commit myself with the desire of doing good and thereby gaining personal satisfaction in the form of self-esteem. That hidden desire is enough to pervert what we are doing, because then we have an attachment, an intention, even though a secret one. It's in this sense that we must understand one of the sayings of the Buddha: 'Abandon the good and, with all the more reason, the bad. The person who reaches the other shore has nothing to do with rafts.'

[†] Curses have been hurled, at all times and in most traditions, at sexual desire, and still more at our desire to satisfy it. The words of the Dalai Lama echo those of saint Augustine, Tertullian, and so many others.

Then we see a feeling of closeness appear. The two individuals who love feel close to one another. Such a rapprochement for her child. This compassion, or affection, is not based on some such idea as, 'This person is close to me, he or she is made for me, we complement one another admirably', or else, 'She is good for me, she does me good, with her my life will be better.' This is a question of a spontaneous affection, free from all calculation.

Still there's the matter of choice. I don't have affection for just anyone, but for this particular person.

Yes, but that affection can expand. Beyond the one person, it can be extended to other individual. If it's truly pure, it won't suffer from any partiality, and it will cease to choose. It can even be applied to our enemies, who, just like us, have the right to suffer.

Buddhism has codified sexual practices after its own fashion. There are correct practices and incorrect practices (such as fellatio, sodomy, masturbation). Homosexuality is not incorrect in itself. It becomes so if it leads to incorrect practices, which is inevitably the case.

Some distinctions that Buddhism makes might surprise us. Thus intercourse with a prostitute, if it follows correct practices, is not blameworthy – provided that the woman is paid by her client. If someone else pays for her, there is a transgression.

For protection against AIDS, Buddhism accepts the use of condoms. But the Dalai Lama never stops saying, even though with a smile, that the best method remains celibacy, chastity.

It's better to renounce – that's what we're always being told, which is at the same time an avowal of defeat, an order to flee. On that point he has nothing new to offer us.

On the other hand he comes back to the subject of love, to that sort of 'clear consciousness' that can develop between two persons, provided there is mutual respect.

Let me put it another way. This compassion can be exercised on two levels. On the first level, the simpler one, I can see others as being like myself. I have no doubt that all human are alike, that they share the same emotions, the same aspirations, the same fears. The differences in physiology (skin colour, slanted eyes, etc.) and culture that appear to separate them, it seems to me, only unify them all the more.

Do you mean that what they have in common is deeper and stronger than what sets them apart?

Much stronger. And it's precisely because they appear to be different that I find their common nature so much more striking. The whole series of racist or racial-cultural theories that the history of the world has seen are absurd and pernicious. They lead to nothing but bloody impasses. Today especially, when images from all over the earth are coming our way, our deep unity seems evident to me. Every new institution ought to take this as its point of departure, as its foundation.

Buddhism has always affirmed its universality.

Exactly.

And the second level?

The second level introduces a notion of reciprocity. We have already talked about this. It consists of saying something that for us is self-explanatory: if I develop hatred toward others, I will be hated in turn, and I will suffer. If instead I develop love and compassion, one day or another I will benefit from it.

The same movement holds true for tolerance.

That's well-known. Fanaticism leads to counterfanaticism, which is just as much to be feared.

Humanity never ceases repeating, ever since it learned how to talk, that violence engenders violence. And it continues to prove how violent it is. It's impossible to break the chain.

I don't think it's impossible. But it is very hard, no doubt. The basis of all moral teaching ought to be the nonresponse to attacks. Of course, compassion and tolerance are only words. And words all by themselves have no force. Our first instinct is always to retort, to react, and sometimes to avenge ourselves, which brings on nothing but more suffering. That's why Buddhism says try experiencing calm. Try it at least once. Meditation can help you to discover tolerance within you. When you have practiced it, you will see how you benefit from it. And hence by your example you can extend it around you.

And if you discover hatred?

Then you haven't searched enough.

In one of your books you write (borrowing from an ancient saying), 'The person who harms you must not be perceived merely as someone who needs your attention, he or she must also be looked upon as your spiritual guide. You will see that your enemy is your supreme teacher.'

I especially like that vision of the enemy as the supreme guru – even though such an attitude seems very hard to attain.

Our enemy offers us a precious opportunity – to better ourselves.

Without enemies would we grow weaker? Would we lose some quality?

Undoubtedly.

Then the more enemies we have, the better we are?

With all the enemies we have, by now we must surely be incomparable! [laughs]

That effect of reciprocity that you speak of is something we find expressed in the Mahabharata *in a single phrase, which some commentators place at the very center of the work, like a diamond from which everything radiates.*

What phrase?

'The Dharma, *when it is protected, protects; when it is destroyed, it destroys.'*

I understand.

If that mysterious law really exists, if the cosmic order depends upon our actions, or as Buddhist teaching says, each action has a consequence in this life or another, aren't we tempted to act with a purpose? Tempted to act to get some benefit from our action?

But that desire is natural! Completely natural! And if it leads us to an action that is better, higher, more thoughtful, so much the better.

So a desire can have good in it?

Of course. When Sakyamuni affirms that our desires, necessarily unsatiated as they are, contribute to keeping us in an imperfect view of the world, that doesn't mean that all desires are to be banished.

He himself was animated by the very ardent desire to have his teaching heard.

It was more than a desire, it was a necessity, born of his compassion. Let's understand this: a desire can be negative or positive. Even if I desire the acquisition of a personal good – let's say health if I'm sick, a bowl of rice if I'm famished – that desire is perfectly justified. The same thing goes for egoism.

There's a positive egoism?

Of course. In most cases the affirmation of the ego leads only to disappointment, or else to conflict with other egos just as exclusive as mine. Especially when the strong development of the ego leads to whims and demands.

We've heard about some strange examples of that in movie stars.

Elsewhere, too. The illusion of the permanent self secretes a danger that lies in wait for all of us. I want this, I want that. You might end up killing someone, as we all know well. The excess of egoism leads to uncontrollable perversions, which always end badly.

At the edge of madness.

But from another standpoint, a firm ego, sure of itself, can be a very positive element. We were talking about the environment, about defending the earth. It's clear that if I decide to carry on that great struggle to save the planet, I have to be sure of myself. Without a very strong sense of self – that is, of its qualities, its possibilities, its conviction – no one can take on such a responsibility. You have to have a real confidence in yourself, that's perfectly clear to me.

Confidence that, under the best of circumstances, can lead to this conviction: since I can do it, I have to do it.

Exactly. If I can return for a moment to the *bodhisattva*, who for us is the ideal being, the one who can lay claim to *nirvana*, to absolute repose in the light, but who refuses to attain it, who prefers to remain in contact with this suffering world to come to its aid. In other words, the *bodhisattva* will not be able to find his or her rest as long as a trace of suffering subsists in the world. It's not enough to be a regular reader of the sutras! It's not enough to ask where is this or that *bodhisattva*? In what direction do I have to prostrate myself? What do I have to say to him?

This *bodhisattva*, we have to produce him or her in ourselves. If I tell myself, with conviction, that my task is to put myself at the service of others, for an unspecified period of time, which might not even have an end, that calls for full and complete determination. Without a very strong ego, such determination remains impossible.

But how many dangers constantly threaten that force of the ego? I'm reminded of an anecdote about the superior of a convent in seventeenth-century Spain, a man ambitious for sanctity, extremely harsh to others and himself, and who said one day, 'For myself, when it comes to humility, I'll take on anyone.'

This determination is the combination of two desires: to help others and to attain the Buddha-state.

The second might appear to be egotistical.

In a certain sense, yes. That's why we think so highly of the attitude of the *bodhisattva*, who renounces bliss.

Because you can't lay claim to the two desires?

Not at the same time. If a being of high quality decides to place himself at the service of others, he renounces the Buddha-state. He needs all his energy, all his learning. How could a mother without hands pull her child from the river? If one day we reach the Buddha-state, we will also be able to help fully, but in a different way, by attaching ourselves more particularly to those with whom we have been in close contact. Starting out from this first circle, the will to help all beings, without exception, expands and spreads.

So we are bearers of that desire.

Yes, all of us, even if it remains secret. We call that feeling *maitre*, which is often translated as 'love'. But once again there's nothing sentimental about this. It's a concrete disposition to help others. 'May all creatures be happy,' Sakyamuni said. Something prompts us to contribute to that universal happiness. We have to discover this *maitre* and put it to work.

Is that the privilege of the Buddha-state?

It's the very nature of the Buddha-state. Two desires meet here: to help all creatures and, with this firmly established goal, to reach the Buddha-state. Thus we arrive at the 'mind of wakefulness', which we call *bodhicitta*.

So awakening is inseparable from compassion?

Absolutely inseparable. All activities that benefit others are acts that reinforce the mind.

And the possibility of that awakening is found in each one of us?

Like compassion. Without exception.

Another definition of this wakeful mind tells us: 'Wait for the awakening to the advantage of others.' Here we are no doubt at the most secret heart of Buddhism, which inseparably mixes fulfillment of being and universal compassion. A large effort of reflection focuses on this precise point, closely linking two notions that seem heterogeneous to us. For, on the one hand, in other traditions we meet a thousand examples of fulfilled saints, that is, with God, in his paradise, after a life of total oblivion of this world and even thanks to that oblivion. This allows the blessed one to concentrate on God alone, on 'real life', 'the true kingdom', which do not belong to the world here below.

On the other hand, we may know charitable individuals, perfectly devoted to others, but who have neglected their own personal fulfillment.

Right from the start, in the first sermons of Prince Siddhartha (one who had personally known the two extremes), it was clear that he rejected equally both the worldly path and the path of renunciation and asceticism. Thus his famous sermon of Benares speaks of a *middle way*, 'which gives vision and knowledge, which leads to peace, to learning, to awakening, and to *nirvana*.' This way is immediately defined by the eight paths that make it up, which it is imperative to follow: 'Right vision, right thought [or resolution], right words, right action, right livelihood, right attention, right concentration.'

The Buddha goes on to the four fundamental truths, of which the first is the truth of suffering (the three others being the cause of suffering, the cessation of suffering, and the way that leads to this cessation). The link between personal perfection and the reality of suffering is thus solemnly established. That link will never again be called into question. On the contrary, all the major commentators on Sakyamuni would strive, and strive still, to tighten it. To becomes better is to help others.

What is the Buddha-state?

The first answer which might occur to one is obvious. It's impossible to put it into words, words being as imperfect and deceptive as they are. Indian and Chinese tradition have always shown great caution with regard to definitions. The best definitions are those that don't fall into the net of words.

Yet to get some access to the Buddha-state, one might at most speak of 'something' that is produced, that is eternal and universal, and of which 'no trace subsists'. But it is clear that this something consists in 'freeing one's mind and those of others'.

Zen Buddhism has particularly insisted on the fact that this illumination is a phenomena so natural and so simple that we have no indication that we have become Buddha. And yet we are in contact with the supreme truth – a truth we have been gradually approaching in our conversation – the truth of emptiness.

The Buddha nature is in each of us; it resides in every living creature and even in every atom. The impurities that we can accumulate in our different existences might obscure it, but they can't destroy it. As Nāgārjuna wrote:

> *As a metal ornament stained with impurity*
> *must be purified by fire,*
> *When it is placed in the fire,*
> *The impurities are burned away but not the ornament.*
> *In the same way in what concerns the mind*
> *Whose nature is clear light,*
> *But which is soiled by the impurities of desire,*
> *The impurities are burned away by the fire of wisdom,*
> *But its nature, the clear light, remains.*

So the mind, the greatest force in the universe, can escape all the contaminations, it can become better (or worse), it can lead itself to the Buddha-state by recognizing and cultivating the Buddha nature that abides unchangeably in itself.

The Buddha nature is therefore a common individual potential to realize, but it is not in itself the Buddha-state. The Buddha-state is the end of all illusion, the cessation of all suffering, the knowledge of all the details of the world, the announcement that entry into *nirvana* is now possible. It is the point at which everything becomes clear and peaceful.

Shantideva describes the mind of awakening:

> *It is the sublime nectar*
> *To destroy sovereign death,*

The inexhaustible treasure
To eliminate the misery of the world.

Then the mind is reunited with the very mind of the Buddha, that substance called 'subtle mind,' which has no beginning or end, which is independent of the body and the brain and is undoubtedly the true cause of consicousness. This subtle mind, which is free of all attachments, has totally eliminated the obstacles that opposed the vision 'of the ultimate nature of all existence'.

For twenty-five centuries poets and thinkers have long spoken about what can't be written. Yet it is only experience that counts. As Shantideva asked, 'Can a sick person be cured simply by reading a medical text?' One can affirm that the path is long, that the modifications which take place in us require time and patience, and that the awakening isn't always clearly perceptible. After all, different schools have proposed different ways all of which stop short at the ineffable, at the region of dark light and silence. All duality disappears, the world and we cease to be two. It becomes clear that language, which is spoken and heard, is necessarily based in some way on the separation between the one who speaks and the one who listens.

To quote a fine Chinese poem from the Middle Ages, attributed to Seng Ts'an (whose awakening is said to have simultaneously cured him of leprosy) and entitled 'Faith in Mind':

Authentic mind: not two
Not two: authentic mind
All discourse ceases.
No more comings and goings now.

Those who claim that all desire is negative are mistaken. They often assign too much importance to notions such as forgetfulness of self and detachment, which leads them to excesses, for example, to never thinking about themselves.

Self-esteem is often too high, can it also be too low?

Yes, it risks linking up with self-hatred, which is a surprising phenomenon.

But more widespread than one might believe. What do you think of psychoanalysis?

Even though Buddhism has known about the unconscious for a very long time, psychoanalysis isn't one of our customs. Perhaps it's a cultural phenomenon, adapted to the West. In any case, it's very interesting. But Buddhism likes to base itself on direct experiences. That's not the case with me and psychoanalysis. I have never done it, and so I hesitate to talk about it.

While Buddhism has a passion for the structure and function of the mind, the same obsession is present in the West today.

But from a different point of view.

Have you met any brain specialists?

Yes, several times.

Since science realized that all research is inseparable from the mind that observes and analyzes, it's supremely important to get to know that mind. To know it we have to study the brain, where we see the locus of thought.

Yes, I know. No one can deny that the brain and the mind are connected. That's evident. But Buddhism doesn't say that all thought and consciousness are necessarily bound up with the molecules of the brain. We distinguish several levels of consciousness. The highest level transcends its material underpinnings. For that reason this consciousness is indestructible.

In your view, does thought/consciousness exist outside the underpinning of the body?

At a certain level, yes. Without a doubt. It is independent of the physical particles.

This is an ancient debate. In the last ten years it has sharpened, and a consensus still hasn't been reached. A rather large number of neurobiologists seem to back the idea that the brain is the sole producer of consciousness and thought. But the spiritualist tradition, which separates the mind (or the soul) from corporeal matter, is far from extinguished, even among scientists. The psychoanalysts resist, of course; and so do some psychiatrists and sociologists.

For three years I worked with a number of actors under the direction of Peter Brook to put together a show called *The Man Who*. We began background research with the work of English neurologist Oliver Sacks, and spent a long time, in New York, Delhi, and Paris, visiting various neurology centers. The doctors introduced us to patients suffering various cerebral lesions, which cause mental illness, aphasias, and amnesia, as well as unclassifiable behaviours that were long considered peculiar, but which are now studied on the basis of specific lesions.

In the course of those visits we saw that the brain and the sense organs can fall completely afoul of each other. One individual who could in no way be considered 'insane' hears imaginary voices distinctly singing songs he had forgotten since early childhood. Some patients don't recognize their arm or leg as their own and try to tear it off and throw it away. Someone else imagines, with perfect conviction, that he lives in a dream, that the hospital and everyone in it are the products of a dream, from which he hopes to wake by climbing up on the roof and flinging himself into space. Another, when presented with a rose, perfectly describes the stalk, the leaves, and the petals but is incapable of saying the word 'rose'. Still another continuously lights and puts out a candle, simply because he sees matches nearby. Another sees only the right side of the image before his eyes, although both eyes are in excellent condition. He eats only the right half of his slice of ham, he shaves only the right side of his face. The list of such cases never ends.

All these aberrant behaviours come from visible lesions. Perhaps such lesions can explain the many illuminations and possessions that we see throughout history. But is that to say that all our behaviours are explainable by the simple workings of our brain?

The brain still remains the great unknown. At the moment we know very little about the functioning of our 100 billion brain cells. The immunologist Gerald Edelman supposes the possibility of an evolution, a sort of natural selection of neurons. Others even talk about the brain as a sort of social organism: they identify this or that type of neuron; they see in them attractions, external influences, combinations, and repulsions; they recognize leaders, networks – so why not sects?

In the realm of particle physics, there is much which seems to run counter to traditional beliefs. On the one hand, the neurobiologists tell us that the mind dies, or in any event seems to fade away and die (nobody has ever been able to find the substance of the mind). But on the other hand the physicists assure us that the matter of our bodies, at its most elementary level (i.e., the particles), does not and cannot die. Our particles are reconstituted in other bodies which in their turn will be able to know what we call death.

And the number of these particles is so high that every time we breathe we take in a few particle of Socrates, of his clothes, of the onions he ate. And not just of Socrates and Julius Caesar, but of all the millions and millions of anonymous men and women who have walked this earth, made up of the same elementary matter that is indefatigably passed on from one to another. Thus, each time he breathes in, the Dalai Lama inhales some particles that formed, temporarily, the Buddha Sakyamuni himself. I too breathe in some of them, and so do all the inhabitants of the earth.

Our elementary matter is immortal, but our mind and our consciousness very much seem to die when the brain stops.

So, contemporary science appears to reverse the ancient data that judged matter to be perishable and the soul immortal?

Yes indeed, speaking cautiously. While some scientists take a radical line here, others prefer to talk about their uncertainty and even their ignorance. To the question, what happens to the mind after death? They generally reply, we don't know.

That is a scientific attitude.

More precisely they say, we lose track of the mind, we don't see it anymore, we can no longer say that it survive the brain.

But perhaps one day they will know?

They hope so. In any case, they persevere in their research. They say they're just beginning.

Buddhists will always be ready to listen to them.

And to change their minds?

Why not?

It's often said in Buddhist Scriptures that the hand can't grasp the hand, that the eye can't see the eye. Can the mind study itself?

That's a difficult question. Can the mind even *see* the mind? We have to answer yes and no. No, because the mind can't be a subject and an object at the same time. We have already spoken about this. I believe that East and West are more or less agreed on this point. The mind interferes, whether it wants to or not, whether it knows it or not, in all that it observes; and with all the more reason when it's a question of itself. But the mind can't see itself completely. Strictly speaking, that's impossible.

Even if one mind observes another mind?

Even in that case. You're alluding to the Western method, based on systematic observation and experiment. To be sure, it gets results, just as psychiatry and psychoanalysis do. All these approaches are valuable, but partial.

They are like armies besieging the same fortress with different machines.

But it's always the mind that's observing the mind, and that wants to observe it in its totality. *We* think that it's better to start out from the inside of the fortress, and proceed gradually, by different zones.

By different levels.

That's it. And this technique is partly feasible. For example, today my mind can remember my mind of yesterday, its thoughts, its questions, its beliefs. In other words, in a certain measure I can *see*, I can read the state in which my mind found itself yesterday. It's a beginning that might take me rather far.

Throughout its long history Buddhism has come to distinguish several hundred thousand, I think, operations of the mind.*

Nobody can claim to know all those operations. A lifetime wouldn't be enough.

Many lifetimes wouldn't be enough. But there, too, several levels of work are possible.

This immense enterprise strikes me as unique in the history of thought. It seems to me that we are missing something: the tranquil observation of the mind as such. We almost never see anything like this in the history of Christianity, where the human mind never puts itself in the position of being an object of thought. At most I can cite Saint

---

* The Dalai Lama was not very sure of this estimate and asked his translator, Lhakdor, to confirm it, which he did.

Thomas Aquinas, who studied the 'agent intellect', distinguishing two functions in the intelligence, one active, the other passive. There are also the Spiritual Exercises of Ignatius of Loyala, where the mind subjects itself to self-discipline, following a careful method, to attain a higher degree of devotion.

There are a number of reasons for that. In the first place, the importance you give to faith and to a creator god. When faith takes hold of us, when we accept a 'credo', there's no longer any reason to examine the mind.

By contrast, when it is the only captain on board ship, when everything depends on its experience, it becomes indispensable to know it.

Absolutely indispensable. In the hypothesis (which is not ours) of a creator god, the permanent judge of our acts, the role of the mind is reduced. We have to dismiss every sort of doubt and questioning. Faith comes to us directly from God; and faith takes us directly to compassion or, if you prefer, to a moral attitude. In that case, it makes no sense to try to deepen the feeling of compassion, to get lost in pointless complications.

And even dangerous for faith.

Naturally. All reflection is dangerous to faith.

And all faith is dangerous for the mind, which sees itself condemned to idleness. Neurologists often talk about the reductive aspect of our brain, which is always willing to be seduced by an easy solution, which is often wrong – though that doesn't stop the brain from clinging to it. Buddhist tradition tells us exactly the same thing in different words. You have to admit that this tradition doesn't always escape the automatic dictatorship of a catechism, of a repetitive formalism, where the mind gets sluggish and easily satisfied.

And yet the Buddha has given us the best possible example. Nowadays we take him to be a superior being, who arrived at the highest conceivable degree of consciousness and existence. But in the beginning, before his awakening and his forty-years of preaching, he was a man like others. It was by his own effort, by his own dogged application, that he became the Buddha.

❖

After leaving the city of Kapilavastu on a magical night while all the palace slept, Prince Siddhartha first decided to lead a wandering life. He was twenty-nine. He cut off his long hair, traded clothes with a poor hunter, and sent back his coachman, Chandaka. Then, he set off in search of a master, begging for rice as he went along. He first followed the teaching of the well-respected Aruda Kalama, then that of Rudraka Ramaputra. He easily matched these two master, but without attaining what he was looking for. He was, however, impressed by the ascetical practices of the holy men he met, and he resolved to adopt that approach. He followed this practice so rigorously for six years that he became completely enfeebled.

Though nearly dead, he still wasn't getting to liberation. He came back to the world, began eating one light meal a day, and finally received illumination. But he didn't receive it completely all at once. Each day his new learning was discussed and challenged, chiefly by himself. The legend tells of Mara, the chief demon, constantly tormenting to turn him away from his work. We also have sketchy reports of divisions among his disciples, and even of the rebellion by one named Devadatta, who wanted to assassinate the Enlightened One so he could take his place at the head of the burgeoning community.

During the forty-five years of his search he never stopped questioning himself, putting his disciples on guard, refining his teaching, and trying to forestall a divinization that he sensed was on the way (and which the Hindus in fact proclaimed, equating Sakyamuni to the ninth incarnation of Vishnu). This means that until the very instant of his entry into *nirvana* his prodigiously developed mind didn't stop working, observing itself, and raising itself to the finest degree of subtlety. Then what can we say about the work to be done on *our* minds?

What is nirvana? *It is often spoken of, but I don't think many have an adequate understanding of what it is. I know that it is not heaven as we conceive it, nor the complete cessation of life, a sort of fading away into the hypothetical Great All. I know too that the first Western commentators on Buddhism spoke of it as an 'abyss of atheism and nihilism', of 'annihilation' and quite simply of 'nothingness'.*

By the very fact that the one who has penetrated into nirvana *is incapable of describing it,* nirvana *remains an enigma. Buddhist commentators mostly speak of escaping the fated cycle of rebirths, of passing into a mode of existence without conditioning, without becoming, without disappearance, finally liberated from the law of impermanence and change. They often acknowledge the impotence of words to express what by definition transcends expression: a superhuman experience.*

Nirvana *is most often defined negatively (absence or cessation of this or that phenomenon), although in itself it is neither positive nor negative, because it transcends both those notions. It even goes beyond the chain of cause effect. Like the supreme truth, it is not produced by anything.*

By the way, the Buddha scarcely spoke of *nirvana* at all. Yes, he did indicate that there was a deliverance from the cycle of rebirths (which, parenthetically, doesn't make the idea understandable to Westerners unless they admit the chain of transmigrations, *samsara*, as a fact) but his indications stop there. So we have a multitude of interpretations. You ask me what *nirvana* is. I would answer: *a certain quality of mind.*

How can one attain that quality?

Human nature is contaminated. The relationship we have with what we call reality has been warped. We must always return to this point: that this relationship is fundamentally erroneous, that it rests on an illusion – those are facts we can't admit unless we escape from this very illusion.

The characteristic of an illusion is that we take it for reality.

Exactly. And it *is* possible to escape from this illusion, as shown by many examples, beginning with Sakyamuni. The contamination must be driven from our minds, and it can be, as we know. Beginning with that purification, with that awakening, our minds can reach the high quality that I call *nirvana.*

So, it isn't necessary to die to get there?

Absolutely not. Besides all our tradition maintains that this high quality of mind is not affected by death. There are many sages who have reached *nirvana* in this life.

From the beginning of our conversations, I have been fascinated above all by this permanent trust in the mind. It seems that nothing can change it, and that the mind, which is capable of the best and the worst, holds within itself its own destiny and by the same token the destiny of the whole world, to which it is intimately connected.

But that connection, close as it may be, doesn't make the mind the prisoner of the world or, if you wish, of matter. By a special effort it can liberate itself, awaken, and survive.

How to be liberated? The heart of the Buddhist method is mediation. In this practice, though, you've said that the physical procedures recommended, concerning posture or the rhythm of breathing, are secondary. Is yoga, then, not useful?

That depends upon the individual – which is an answer Buddhism often gives. For some people yoga is difficult and painful, and doesn't help the mind's work at all. For others it's a simpler and more natural method, which can contribute to their general well-being. But [and here he insists], *the principal tool for purifying the mind is the mind itself.*

If we pay heed to our desire, if we pay some attention to the workings of our mind, we can't help being amazed to discover its importance. It is at the center of everything.

You have said that it has to be our own policeman.

And our judge, absolutely. And it has all the means for this. Buddhism affirms that man is his own master, in any event he has the possibility of becoming it. That's the very foundation of Buddhist philosophy, and we have tested a large number of techniques to arrive at that mastery.

Which is the work of the mind?

Of what else? The mind is its own creator at every instant. Hence its responsibility, which is essential.

If the mind realizes that it is its own creator, and puts that power into practice, I suppose that our attitude changes immediately and totally?

That's the goal. The only goal.

6

Between Exile and the Kingdom

It seems to me that the twentieth century has been the century of exile. It's often been characterized differently, by the total wars, by the holocausts, by the technological progress that we have discussed. But people frequently forget about the exile, voluntary or forced, of tens of millions of individuals, having to pass inspection on Ellis Island before being admitted to the United States, colonial soldiers drafted against their will, immigrant workers demanded by Europe, which today rejects them, displaced populations like the Vietnamese boat people, and others too numerous to mention. Never did any one century tear up so many roots.

I hadn't thought of it, but it's undoubtedly true.

Yet we know that there is a profound link between a people and its land, and that this tie is the origin of a thousand customs, behaviours, and even beliefs.

Yes, that's certain.

Still here and there we have undertaken to cut that link. You yourself have been living in exile for thirty-five years. The Chinese invaded Tibet in 1950, when you were fifteen. For nine years, you tried to resist, to negotiate. You met Mao Ze-dong and Jou En-lai. You made appeals to other powers, but it was all in vain. China wouldn't stop laying on Tibet the burden of increasingly harsh oppression, from massacres to colonization. Then you reached the decision to leave your country and your people to continue your struggle abroad, according to your method.

That's right.

Has exile helped you? Have you found strength in it?

Oh yes! Without a doubt. I can try to tell you why? When, at some point in our lives, we meet a real tragedy – which could happen to any one of us – we can react in two ways. Obviously we can lose hope, let ourselves slip into discouragement, into alcohol, drugs, unending sadness. Or else we can wake ourselves up, discover in ourselves an energy that was hidden there, and act with more clarity, more force.

You chose the second way?

I hope so. I discovered at the age of fifteen the brutal power of politics. I discovered pitiless imperialism, the cruel desire for conquest, the so-called law of arms. In my youth communism had a certain seductive appeal for me. It even seemed to me that a synthesis between Buddhism and communism was possible. Then

I ran up against the incomprehensible contradictions of Chinese policy – the frenzy of slogans, the intoxication of millions of brains. I got to know all that in my adolescence, in my youth. After which came the disappointments, and finally the certainty, that Mao was none other than the 'destroyer of the Dharma'.

You were only nineteen years old, in 1954, when you learned that India had signed an accord with China with which they abstained from challenging the military occupation of Tibet.

Yes, another disappointment. That one was diplomatic. Around the same time I became aware of the first attacks launched by the Chinese against the Tibetan religion, which they accused of being archaic and barbarous. Some of those attacks were treacherously indirect, such as the extermination campaigns against insects and rats, whereas Buddhism forbids us to kill even an animal.

And the brutality took the political executions?

Yes, the oppressive measures, and the atrocities of every kind, making collaboration impossible. Monasteries destroyed, works of art plundered, crucifixions, vivisections, dismemberments, entrails and tongues ripped out. We experienced all those horrors, and on our soil. In 1959, amid all the confusion, I finally followed the advice of an oracle that had several times advised me to leave; I decided to go into exile.

Thirty-five years later that exile continues.

One positive aspect of the exile situation is that you look at your country differently. Thus, apropos of Tibet, all the ritual that surrounded my youth has lost its importance. From the first day of the year till the last, it was nothing but a long round of ceremonies, perfectly ordered, and which everyone took very seriously. This formalism regulated every last detail of our everyday life. You had to observe it even while talking, even while walking.

Exile has erased the prestige of ritual?

To be sure. The solemn aspect touches me much less. It's inevitable. The flight and all that followed it, our patient struggle to get ourselves recognized by other nations, all my journeys, all my public addresses have brought me closer to reality. It also has to be said that exile has allowed me to discover the rest of the world, to meet other peoples, to become acquainted with other traditions. Nothing could be more useful. India has welcomed us. Our being installed in a free country has facilitated these meetings, which in the 1950s remained difficult in Tibet.

Isn't India a sacred land for Buddhists?

'Yes, it's *Aryabhûmi*, the land where the Buddha Sakyamuni was born for the last time, the land where he experienced illumination, where he preached. We have many centers in India, and every year I'm very moved when I return to Buddh Gaya, to the very spot where he found the awakening.

Has this exile of thirty-five years created a new feeling among the Tibetans?

Yes, undoubtedly. A real 'Tibethood'. It was born from that difficult passage in the long history of Tibet. Centuries and centuries of rootedness can make you forget that feeling. The bonds with the earth seem secure, untouchable. Then something unexpected happens that calls those bonds into question. You discover a cynical brutality, the crushing use of force, your own weakness. Finally you leave, you never see your country except from far away. It gets ravaged, occupied, and still you realize that it hasn't disappeared, that it subsists in you, that you still feel Tibetan. Then you begin to wonder, What does being Tibetan mean?

That no doubt explains all those efforts to open schools, to maintain the Tibetan language, music, song, dance?

We have created a system where all the instruction is given in Tibetan, even in the scientific disciplines.

And that developed the language?

Inevitably, and strengthened our union. We have something to defend. Among our efforts have been literary publications, such as *Jang Chon* ('Young Shoots') and *Tibetan Art and Literature*. After 1959, the Chinese police in Tibet hunted down the creators of that young literature, which they labelled reactionary. Every work had to be authorized for publication by the party cell, and such permits were very hard to get. The pioneer of this literature, the novelist Thondup Gyal, committed suicide in 1985. He was one of those who bitterly criticized the traditions and beliefs of Tibet, which he felt were responsible for the present-day enslavement.

Apropos of Tibet, haven't you spoken in several of your books about a collective karma?

That's an intimate part of our classical teaching. What is true for an individual – who will feel in one of his or her existence the effects, favourable or not, of his or her *karma* – is true for groups, for a family, say, and also for a nation, for a people.

So Tibet had something to 'pay'? This chain of events was inevitable?

One might wonder. For a very long time Tibet cut itself off from the world. It refused all changes, all outside influences. It wanted to believe that it alone possessed the truth, that it could live in isolation.

But the world reminded Tibet that it was there.

Very harshly. And we wonder in fact if our collective *karma* didn't lead us to that confrontation, which ended in disaster.

That would be a subtle form of collective responsibility.

Perhaps.

Do you still believe in it today?

As always in Buddhism, you have to distinguish causes from conditions. The principal causes of aggression, of so many misfortunes and sufferings, have to be looked for in the former lives, and not necessarily among the Tibetans.

Among other peoples?

Perhaps even on other stars, in other galaxies. Everything is connected to everything else. No event can be considered isolated, unrelated to the others. We have already spoken about that. Other sensitive and responsible beings, by their behaviour, have managed to create a negative *karma*, whose effect is felt at that particular moment. This boundless chain of causes and consequences is almost impossible to untangle, but it exists. All our acts have a weight. That weight will make itself felt, one day or another, here or there, individually or collectively. This is a major reason why we should respect the way of the *Dharma*.*

And the conditions?

For the conditions, the Tibetans themselves are certainly responsible.

Out of blindness?

No doubt. Out of ignorance of the rest of the world, of China, India, the political tensions, the upheavals brought on by World War II. Many Tibetans thought that our country was an extraordinary territory transcending the common laws and even the passage of time.

---

* This notion of Dharma is no doubt one of the radical points separating East and West. The position of the individual, of his or her status and rights, and hence the existence of his or her ego – such individualism already exists in Christian tradition. But destinies, even eternal salvation is an individual affair. The idea of a whole nation being condemned to Gehenna or called to Paradise is quite alien to Christianity. The individual always has the possibility of encountering the truth and 'winning salvation' or choosing Hell. The laws of modern republics have only confirmed our capacity to choose.

Here at Dharamsala, an immense effort is demanded of the individual to penetrate into the self, and to seek the inner calm. Despite this practice, no one forgets that he or she is nothing but an unstable substance, continuously made and unmade, with no independent individual existence. For that very reason each sees him or herself related to all the rest of the world.

Because of Buddhism?

Yes, in part, because of the Buddha Dharma. A whole people following the just law and faithfully accomplishing its rituals, necessarily had to guarantee protection for that same people.

Did all the inhabitants of Tibet share that feeling?

Not all of them. A large number, yes. And among them certain high dignitaries, responsible for the defense of the country, who believed in invisible protectors.

Against the perfectly visible aggressors.

This was an aberration, complete blindness in the face of destiny. During the Chinese invasion in 1950, when the young Communist army was crossing our borders, these high dignitaries entrusted our defense to our deities. One official, now deceased, assured me that we had no cause for concern: our gods would protect us from the Chinese.

You were fifteen years old.

And everything disposed me to believe what I was told: my childhood, the way I had been chosen, my meticulous education, my life at Potala, the incense that accompanied my walks. But my eyes were opened very quickly, as you can imagine. In the middle of the twentieth century prayers matched with cannons?

The government put its confidence in the divinities, but on the other hand it ignored the prophecies and the oracles.

The people in charge didn't want to hear them?

The ones responsible weren't responsible.*

Not all Tibetans, however, were living in the same illusion. My predecessor, Thupten Gyatso, the thirteenth Dalai Lama, when he died in 1933, clearly pointed out in his testament that one day communism would pose a terrible danger. He already understood that we could never physically resist our great neighbours, China and India, that we had to use an adroit diplomacy; and so he turned to our small neighbours, Nepal and Bhutan.

What did he propose to them?

A sort of common defense: raise an army, train is as best as possible.

Just between us, this isn't strictly practicing nonviolence.

How did Nepal and Bhutan react?

---

* This discussion certainly did not make the Dalai Lama smile. Oracles, prophecies, and premonitory dreams play an important role in Tibetan tradition even to this day. These oracles are monks, mediums who have received special training. Divinities can become incarnate in their body, transforming their face and voice in a trance, and speaking though their mouth. In this state their face reddens, their eyes become bloodshot, and their tongue gets thick and pendulous. The broken words they utter are received and interpreted by other monks. The most celebrated is the oracle of Nechung, the incarnation of the god Pehar. The Tibetan government employs him in what might be called an official capacity.

The Dalai Lama doesn't seem to doubt the truth of this tradition. He writes that after the death of the grand lamas, their bones melt, and then one can see images in them or read in them letters that indicate which deity is protecting the deceased. Thus we see what can be called 'a supernatural dimension' slipping into a body of thought that aims to be rigorous, and that strives to maintain nothing unless it comes from experience.

It's impossible (and absurd) to pick and choose here. From the most profound analysis to the most naïve belief, all this belongs to the same structure; and at the same time every fiber of the teaching sheds light on all the others.

They didn't react. They quite simply ignored the offer. Now I can see the whole range of my predecessor's vision. For example, he wanted to bring to Lhasa some boys from the region of Kam in the east – it's a harsh territory, thinly populated, close to China – and give them the rank of real Tibetans, with a complete military education. Politically, that was very farsighted. He was already advancing the idea that the defense of a land has to be assured by the people who occupy it.

Then they have to be given arms?

That's what he said. The man felt very keenly the movement of the world around him. He wanted to go with the changes, not leave his country behind, or by the way side.

If that vision had materialized, would Tibet have been able to resist twenty years later?

I'm convinced it would have. But he wasn't listened to. The dignitaries didn't follow his orders. That's what we call the conditions, one could also say the circumstances, of collective *karma*. In the Buddhist conception of action, no event can be isolated, nor produced without a chain of causes, conditions, and consequences. And so we stubbornly seek for the conditions, which are easier to detect than the causes, which are often far removed from the event.

As far back as 1961, the Dalai Lama, who had become what he calls a 'politician despite himself', proposed a constitution which was accepted. Since then he has never ceased presenting and defending, on every occasion, the cause of his country, of his people.

First of all, he passes on information. Thus we have learned about the extermination of more than a million Tibetans (one out of six), repressive measures of all kinds, population transfers, expropriations, internment in concentration camps, brutal application of birth control policy, and forced sterilization of women. Then there is the deforestation, the use of Tibetan territory as a nuclear waste dump, and above all, a systematic Chinese colonization. Nowadays their techniques are being refined: while young Chinese, after three years of military service, must return to their home province, those stationed in Tibet are obliged to stay there. Estimates put the current Chinese population in Tibet at around 9 million, so the Tibetans are now a minority in their own homeland. The Tibetan 'race' is in danger of disappearing.

In the 1960s, the United Nations voted a number of resolutions on Tibet that have remained a dead letter. But little by little the world began to wake up. In 1985, ninety-one members of the U.S. Congress signed a letter of support, addressed to the President of the People's Assembly in Beijing. In 1987, the Dalai Lama himself was invited to Washington to speak before the Committee on Human Rights. Aware of how unrealistic it would be to demand immediate independence, pure and simple, for Tibet, he proposed a 'five point peace plan'.

The plan foresees the transformation of Tibet into a zone of peace, China's abandoning its policy of colonization, respect for democratic freedoms, fundamental human rights for the Tibetan people, the restoration and protection of the environment (to begin with, by stopping all nuclear activity), and, finally, the opening of serious negotiations on the future status of Tibet.

In 1988, before the European Parliament in Strasbourg, he developed and explained these five points. He proposed, in particular, to turn Tibet into a vast demilitarized zone and a sort of natural park, the largest in the world, where environmental restoration would be exemplary. All the international organizations working to defend human rights would have their place in that territory of *ahimsa*, or nonviolence. Separated by a vast neutral region. India and China could withdraw the troops that they continue to maintain, at great expense, in the Himalayan regions.

In 1989, the awarding of the Nobel Prize for peace seemed to reinforce his proposals.

When you received the Nobel Prize many people discovered the problem of Tibet. They picked up maps in order to simply find out where Tibet was located, and furthermore became interested in what was happening between Tibet and China. It must also have with the heads of state around the world.

Naturally. Some received me officially, others privately. Always these diplomatic reasons. In any case, it got easier for me to meet the people in charge and talk to them.

Even the Chinese leaders?

Yes, even with the Chinese, the Nobel Prize played a positive role there too.

Yet when you put forth your proposals, when you set up a ministry, gathered deputies and opened offices in various foreign capitals, the Chinese refused to see anything in all that but reactionary moves and an attempt at 'secession'. The Chinese continue to imprison any Tibetans who show loyalty to you or their traditions. At the *same time, those who support China are rewarded by the occupiers. The exile continues, but from time to time Lhasa is shaken by demonstrations which are immediately repressed. It is said the situation is worse today than ever.**

Tibet has been independent for centuries; it isn't anymore. We have to look things in the eye. We are asking for autonomy, we don't dream of independence anymore. But we don't want to negotiate except on the basis of mutual respect. Conditions today are not those of the past, and we are ready to take our inspiration from the words of Deng Ziaoping: 'One country, two systems.' But the minds of the Chinese aren't going in that direction, not at this moment, anyhow.

I've heard the Chinese are demolishing the old quarters of Lhasa.

Yes, under the pretext that they're unhealthy. The situation is bad.

What can one do? Can international pressure play a role?

It's essential. Above all it must not ease up, because the Chinese sometimes show that they're sensitive to it. Every time I make a public statement, wherever in the world it might be, there are Chinese in the hall. Sometimes I even speak to them, and they know how to behave very agreeably. This attitude does indicate that they're following my activities, that they're interested in what I say, even if in their newspapers they accuse me of all sorts

* The Dalai Lama's assistants suggest that the only chance for an accord would be a severe crisis in China itself. But there is no reason to anticipate one. President Clinton personally intervened in 1993, apparently to no avail. In February 1994, a French newspaper spoke of a project of 'federation', but the Dalai Lama denies the report.

of things. Sometimes they accuse me of personal ambition, of counterrevolutionary thinking, of wanting to restore a theocracy. The classic charges.

Are you optimistic?

Yes. Because Tibet's cause is just. I'm sure of it. And also because China won't be able to remain aloof from freedom forever.

On the one hand the Dalai Lama promotes a vigilant realism, a renewed effort to adapt to this changing world – an effort all the more meritorious because in ancient Tibet, a kingdom of impermanence, things used to seem forever immutable.

On the other hand, the dream persists of a sort of ideal land, beyond the ranges of the Himalayas, like the Shangri-La of *Lost Horizons*, a miraculously protected land, where peace-minded people could meet. A land that would be an example to the world, where Buddhism, free of its ancient formalism, would find its true function of lookout and explorer.

Utopia? It's never certain. The difficult dreams are part of us, too. They draw us and they help us, assuming they don't lead us to a paradise regained. They can bring us to slip a little of Tibet inside each one of us.

Can politics be reconciled with ahimsa?

Yes, that ought to be possible. Why not? Look at our century. It thought up, or worked out, a whole gamut of things to make violence the rule in human relations, from world war, with the destruction of entire cities, to genocide, to institutional torture, to terrorism as a form of action. All these methods have failed, and always will.

Why?

Because they're superficial. They crash against the powerful ground of our nature, which is made of goodness and generosity. Let's take the example of the Israelis, who have gone through forty years of hatred. Even if the extremist groups on both sides continue to chant – and to practice – that vain and bloody hatred, some day or other they'll have to make peace. The promotion of hatred leads to nothing but hatred. Violence is the worst of arbitrators. Mutual respect is inevitable.

At the end of the Mahabharata, *king Yudhisthira finally ascends the throne. He is the very son of Dharma, and consequently called 'Dharmaraj'. For once Dharma itself is king. And under his leadership the world will come to know thirty-six years of peace and prosperity.*

But that perfect direction does not suppose any relaxation of the king's vigilance. If Yudhisthira appears with the Dharma in his right hand, he always holds a rod in his left. And he is ready to use it. That's what the king is there for.

Naturally, but in the world of today, authority must be exercised in the name of the law, under the control of the constitution. And that authority must above all else be benevolent. It must not punish for punishment's sake.

You are opposed to the death penalty?

Absolutely opposed to it. My predecessor abolished it in Tibet. Today I find it unbelievable that it persists in large countries like China and India. In the name of justice they are still killing people in the country of Mahatma Gandhi! In the very land where the Buddha taught! The death penalty is pure violence, a barbaric and useless violence. Dangerous even, because it can only lead to other acts of violence. As all violence does.

So punishment has to be limited to imprisonment?

The supreme punishment ought to be a life sentence, as with you. And without any brutality.

I've noticed that even today in films they never really kill the animals. They tranquilize them with injections, so that they'll look dead. Except in the Chinese movies: there they really do kill them, right out in the open. I've also seen in Chinese scientific films rats with their skulls open. Horrible. And they show that on television.*

Also, the faithful who go on pilgrimage to Mecca have to sacrifice an animal, but at least the sacrifice isn't shown.

I strive as best I can to bring about harmony everywhere. Millions of acts of violence every instant are destroying that harmony. Why add more to the list? Why practice and show violence when it's not inevitable? The slaughter of an animal is an injury to universal harmony. I really have a horror of that.

At this very moment, in Tibet, I'm told that thousands of animals are killed by the Chinese, for simple amusement. Dogs,

* I was tempted to tell him that real death, on the screen, is not the exclusive property of Chinese film directors. In Western films we kill pigs and chickens on the screen. A live ox is cut into pieces in *Apocalypse Now*, and rabbits and patridges are slaughtered en masse in *The Rules of the Game*. There are numerous examples in many other films. If we look close, death, real death, is constantly there.

for example. They cut off a paw, or some other part of the body, or else they strip off the skin, and they let them go around that way till they die. Look at the mentality that's developing there.

Which has to be fought against?

Of course. As you were saying apropos of Dharmaraj, you always have to hold the rod in one hand and make use of it if necessary. Yes, one way or another, there has to be a system of discipline.

Despite the goodness of our nature?

That natural goodness has a lot of trouble manifesting itself.

It's simpler to be cruel.

Simpler for some people, certainly. To be cruel is to stop along the way. It's to give up, for one reason or another, the task of penetrating our own depths. It's remaining attached to our irritated or exasperated surface.

It's pitching the battle on bad terrain.

Precisely. That's why I believe that from infancy onward you have to give the highest place to education. I keep coming back to that. Along with that education there has to be a practice of the mind, in the form of meditation, and if possible the soothing influence of a united family, of a happy marriage.

It's a beautiful dream.

I know that. Still, such harmony exists. We can feel it strongly, sometimes. It's inscribed in the deepest part of us. It's our first tendency. There are, and there always will be evildoers, I know that, too.

And hence the need for the rod?

To be used with as little brutality as possible.

A goodness inscribed in our depths, a fundamental and all-powerful gentleness, without which the whole Buddhist edifice becomes incomprehensible. Goodness that extends to the whole universe, and that will lead us one day to *nirvana*, but a fragile goodness, since the killing of a dog can upset the order of the world. A secret goodness as well, which easily hides beneath arrogance, brutality, and greed – the masks we most often wear.

The apparent paradox – why all the insistence on education, if all we have to do is trust our nature our nature? – is no doubt resolved by the danger that surrounds us, the danger born of the illusion we are born and live in. Our persistent misfortune is surely rooted in this blindness. As soon as it stops, and the awakening occurs, then all things will seem quite normally clam, as if our desires had vanished. At least that's what Buddhism says.

However, if the causes of that 'mentality' can be described in this way (as both collective responsibility and individual perversions), how can its conditions be determined? In other words, do there exist particular circumstances that favour such cruelties?

We discuss once again, this time more rapidly, the topics of overpopulation and poverty, conditions that are recognized and admitted, and against which the struggle is hard. We touch on nationalism, that old source of bloodshed, on the lust for power that suddenly takes hold of this or that group of people and drives them to commit ferocious acts.

Very soon we find ourselves talking about television. I tell him that in the United States for two or three years now there has been sharp criticism voiced about the increase of murders on the screen. These complaints are not new. Before television such criticism was aimed at the movies, theater, painting, and literature – actually, at most forms of expression. Critics accuse them of projecting a mainly vicious and bloody image of the world, especially to the defenseless eyes of children, who tend to view that world as the real one.

To which the defenders of freedom of expression reply, with some very good arguments, that this baneful influence has not been proved, and that no censorship has ever solved a social problem. But it's true that an American or European child witnesses an astonishing rash of on-screen killings every day. Some TV heroes spend most of their time with an automatic pistol in hand, gunning down their fellows. There is good reason for raising questions, and getting worried, about this.

Political and religious leaders ought to admit nowadays that they're no longer the only ones to exercise power, or even authority.

You mean the power of the media?

Yes. The power of the press has been well-known for many years. But today the power of radio, and still more of television has moved front and center.

It's an indirect power.

It doesn't make much difference how it's exercised. Direct or indirect, it's a real power, which acts on us, which modifies our behaviour, our tastes, and probably our thoughts. Like all authority, it can't be applied at random, any which way.

Otherwise that power could become arbitrary.

Obviously. Arbitrary and irresponsible.

Still, we see radio stations and TV channels almost everywhere whose sense of responsibility seems remarkably thin. The people who run those channels say, We're in the business of entertaining. We obey the laws of the market, of competiton.

In other words, these executives refuse to acknowledge that they are exercising power?

That's their essential point. They present their objective as purely commercial; their only ambition being to raise the rating. In certain cases the means employed don't matter much, and any moral preoccupations are set aside.

That's serious mistake. The people who run those channels, and the ones who finance them, exercise power whether they want to or not. That power gives them a responsibility comparable to religious or political responsibility. In their own way they contribute to the establishment and maintenance of a human community. The well-being of that community should be their first concern.

On that point I have a few doubts.

But the problem has been posed, and for a long time now.

Yes, all over the world governments are wondering about it; overseeing committees are set up, TV consumer organizations protest, laws are passed but they often contradict one another. Nobody has yet found the magic formula, perhaps because no one on the decision-making level dares attack the problem head-on.

How do you see this problem?

In no way am I a partisan of some moral order, or of vigilant censorship. Quite the contrary. But I can see, just as you do, that nowadays the programming directors of TV channels have as much real power as, if not more than, the government. So I find myself wondering, like many people, about the torrents of vulgarity and violence that television regales us with.

One large problem with all this is that children spend more hours in front of the TV set than in their classrooms. Some feel they are discovering the world, but it isn't the real world, it's only an image of the world.

But can't one say that their knowledge has become more extensive?

Yes. Children who have been deprived of television sometimes show real gaps in their learning.

So what worries you is their passivity? You can answer a teacher, you can interrupt and question, even challenge him or her. But how do you talk to an object?

The TV set is brought in among us almost like a new member of the family. It has become an integral part of our lives. And not only do we look at it, but the next day at work or at school we talk about what we saw the night before. It becomes a sort of circle, an airtight chamber – it is at the point where television makes programmes that refer to nothing but itself.

And that forget the world?

That forget and distort it.

That depends upon the programmes. The media can give a euphoric or, on the contrary, a very negative picture of the earth. And I imagine that people wind up looking at the world in that false form.

Yet, the image wins out over the reality. The 'representation' triumphs. The world ends by resembling what we see on television.

If we get superabundance of violent images from it, we end up believing that the world is like that.

That's how we see it.

As a result we are convinced that human nature is aggressive.

It must be admitted that what we learn about real events – on TV news, for example – can only confirm that feeling. No journalist knows what 'good news' is. The selection of items they present us with every day is all murders and attempted murders, accidents, confrontations, fraud, natural disasters. With all this it's not surprising to hear of TV viewers having nervous breakdowns from information overload. Fictional TV shows alongside the news can only drive the nail in all the way.

Yes, but it's well-known that good feelings only cause boredom, and gently put you to sleep. Sometimes it might be good to show a crime.

In what sense?

Since we have a natural compassion in us, and that compassion has to manifest itself, it might be good to awaken it. Violence done to an innocent person, for example, can make us indignant, scandalize us, and in so doing help us to discover our compassion. By its very violence television might keep us in a state of alert.*

Some who study the influence of television tend to say the opposite, that it only aggravates our indifference.

How?

Because everything is presented there on the same level of interest. Now it seems to me that if our mind is to be impressed by an event and remember it long afterwards, it needs to distinguish it from other events.

Yes. Whether for good or for evil.

Uniformity leads to forgetfulness. That's why some observers call TV a 'forgetting machine', because it puts everything on the same level.

* I'm a little surprised to see the Dalai Lama defend, from a strictly Buddhist point of view, a certain form of public violence. A little before this he was, on the contrary, denouncing the visible suffering and death of animals, as if it was important not to *show* it. Now, at least on the subject of violence done to human beings, his attitudes seems to be more flexible.

Even fiction and reality increasingly tend to blend there. And that's not just true for children.

If the violence leads to compassion that's a good thing. If the accumulation of violence leads to indifference, that is very dangerous.

Then there are the strange drifts of language. In the same way that many confuse spiritual life and religious life, a large part of the public confuses violence and action. An action film is a violent film. Often, needless to say, with sex too. How could sex, which is also becoming increasingly violent, awaken compassion?

I don't know. How one tells the difference, between what in the media is ultimately good and bad for the general harmony of the world, I honestly don't know. But I see clearly that the problem exists.

The temptation to indifference, where we both see a danger, is something I sometimes feel in myself. Back in the '60s or '70s, when people told me sad stories – and there was no shortage of them, all around us – I felt very moved, I often cried. Little by little those stories have become familiar to me, my emotion has subsided, and my tears have dried up out of habit.

That happens to us all.

In my youth, when I lived at Lhasa, I used to see the butchers taking the animals to the slaughterhouse. As I was extremely sensitive to the fate of animals, and I had a little money, I bought cattle and sheep to save them, to set them free. But then there was quite a problem: where to put the survivors?

I had made arrangements that every time a liberated animal died, its body had to be brought to Potala to feed the dogs.

Otherwise, anybody could secretly kill it, declare it dead, and eat it or even sell it.

Wasn't that a bit naïve? The butchers just kill the number of animals needed for consumption.

It was undoubtedly rather naïve, but I was twelve or thirteen then. What I mean is that I've lost the feeling that inspired me in my youth. Today in India I go here and there, I see animals condemned to death, thousands and thousands of chickens, for example, and sometimes I ask myself: I could buy some of them and save them, but where to put them? Who would take care of them?

I could, of course, recite a mantra or say a prayer. What else? Here, too, habit has changed my attitude. This, by the way, is a central point of outreaching: how to reach nonattachment without falling into indifference.

In discussions of violence very often Aristotle's notion of catharsis comes up. Catharsis is a purgation. According to Aristotle, provided that a tragedy is inspired by lofty sentiments (an indispensable condition), it can bring about this purgation by showing or telling about violent actions, freeing the spectators from their aggressive instincts, and sending them home calmer and better prepared for life.

This positive influence of tragic and possible violent action is purely a theatrical matter. Now the theater is always a fiction, it doesn't aspire to be reality. As we all know, the actors don't really die. In the movies and on TV, however, this relationship is overturned. Here we have a connected series of photographs; and a photograph always shows us something that at a certain moment did exist. Thus *movies and TV are, by the very technique that they use, realistic, if not real, expressions.**

Does the effect of catharsis continue to apply in a realistic genre? For example, does a TV news programme full of images of war, famine, and gangland executions leave us more peaceful and self-confident?

Often it all depends on our personal convictions. If we are rather optimistic, open, and in favour of movement, we tend to be indulgent. We reassure ourselves. We say, it's better that the violence be a spectacle outside of us, so the images can free us from our own horrors. If, however, we're conservatives, closed and drawn to the stability of institutions and sentiments, we revolt saying, all this just shamefully plays with our troubles and awakens things in us that ought to be dormant.

No doubt that's what causes attempts at censorship.

There have been many such attempts in the history of film. At the end of the 1920s all of Hollywood obeyed a strict code which spelled out precisely what was possible to say and show. But the code broke down very quickly.

In any case, it's difficult to impose censorship in a democracy. Though we can still see censorship at work in India. Real violence and even explicit eroticism are permitted in Indian films. Women can display themselves very provocatively, as they do everywhere else. Yet until recently men and women never kissed on the lips. People killed one another, but they didn't kiss. And yet it's more agreeable to kiss than to kill!

* The Dalai Lama, who always paid close attention, appeared particularly interested by this distinction, which he grasped immediately.

In Indian films, most of the time we witness the development of a love story, which meets violent opposition, but in the end the good-hearted people are reunited and rewarded, while the villains are punished.

In the history of cinema, films have seldom dared to present a perfectly happy criminal at 'The End'. In this we have submitted to a sort of tacit self-censorship, even if there are a thousand ways of twisting it. The real criminal in the movies is almost always unmasked and punished. On the other hand, there's often a long list of innocent victims despoiled and assassinated.

Nevertheless, for simple souls no doubt there is a good use for television. I see a man commit a crime, then the man is arrested by the police, he goes on trial, and he gets sent to prison. Often he's shot dead by the police. In any event, he pays for what he's done.

It's a very simple scheme, which actually can work in certain cases. But other critics say that the mere story of a burglary, or a hostage-taking or a political murder can awaken vocations for crime.

That's why real discipline can come only from within. If I see a criminal punished by the police, that might in fact dissuade me. But I might also tell myself that if I'm clever or lucky enough, I could escape the police.

Whereas one never escapes karma.

Exactly. Whatever we do, in this life or in another, the weight of *karma* will catch up with us. If that conviction comes home to us, the danger of television will seem less formidable.

Since the origins of Buddhism, the theory of nonviolence has never been presented without some restrictions. And the example was set by the Buddha Sakyamuni himself. Having embarked one day on a boat that was crossing a river, and seeing a bandit who was threatening the lives of other passengers, he chose to sacrifice the life of the bandit. This precedent, coming from such a high source, is frequently quoted. It also has to be handled with care, since we all know how easy it is to call someone a bandit, thereby finding a pretext for suppressing him.

In the same way, during the great war of the *Mahabharata*, where all life is at stake, it happens that the deceptions and outright lies of Krishna (the earthly incarnation of the god Vishnu) scandalize even his own friends. At a certain moment, surrounded by incomprehension, Krishna is led to say (though in a low voice and as secretly as possible) that to defend the *Dharma* you sometimes have to forget the *Dharma*. The line is fraught with a thousand perils: any dictator could borrow it for his own purposes, speaking (as they always do) of a state of emergency, of danger to the homeland, in short, of a situation so critical that all the formalities of the law must be suspended. Just for a moment, of course. But these moments often last a whole lifetime.

What to do then? How can one deal with the violence that we all feel within us and that we see all around us?

Perhaps what we have here is another unexplained view, another question with no answer.

Real discipline isn't imposed. It must come from within ourselves. And, to begin with, this means those who make the films and those who show them. The first have become aware of their responsibilities, which are heavier than ever.

Because the films are distributed all over the world.

And because they have to act in a broader interest. It's indispensable. Perhaps also some sort of connection ought to be worked out between the people who make the films and the people who watch them.

Yes, because right now it's a one-way street, with only one rule, unfortunately a commercial one: make what pleases the largest number. That holds true inside any one country, but also from one country to another. For example, the United States distributes a lot of movies and TV shows to the rest of the world, but it receives almost nothing from the outside.

People use the pretext of simple commercial rivalry, subject to the laws of the market (but what laws? Decreed by whom? And in the name of what?). But I have no doubt that this is a new type of colonization. I've found the same sort of phenomenon in the Chinese occupation of Tibet. The pretext there wasn't commercial, but political, and even cultural. They announced that they were bringing us the revolution, new and luminous times. In reality, the propaganda merely disguised as appetite for hegemony.

Certain distributors in the United States talk about a sort of image monopoly, which they would seriously like to set up over the rest of the world. In India, for example, they'll soon be distributing dubbed American films to compete with Indian cinema in its own market. When these distributors say this you have to see that they will also be pushing through their other products along with films: cars, clothes, drinks, music, everything that constitutes the American way of life. This no doubt includes, though it's less obvious, ways of behaving and thinking.

I'm quite familiar with that method and I'm as much afraid of it as you are. The vehicles it employs are seductive, often above suspicion. Who can detect exactly what is disguised in a film?

It seems to me that the image we keep hearing so much about isn't a superficial phenomenon. Every image, even a fleeting and clumsy one, is the reflection of a profound reality, which would not have appeared without it. In the next century the people who fail to get the means to fashion their own images will be threatened with disappearance.

I'm entirely of that opinion.

For part of my travels around India I had a car and driver – a forty-three-year-old Sikh man with a jet-black beard, a bit plump, and very cordial. One night in Delhi he invited me to dinner with a bus driver associate of his. He cooked a rather good chicken curry himself which, with a bottle of potent Indian rum, we ate in the car.

He talked to me a little about his life. His father lost both his legs in the war between India and Pakistan. He himself was born in Delhi, got married, had children, opened a restaurant. When Indira Gandhi was assassinated by one of her Sikh guards, part of the population of Delhi took revenge on the Sikhs. He lost his restaurant, his apartment, even one of his children. He wound up living on the streets, looking for work. He eventually took the job as a chauffeur with a rental agency. He works hard and hopes one day to have enough money to open another restaurant.

Since I didn't need him at Dharamsala, I let him make the all-night bus ride to Amritsar to see some of his family. He came back four days later, very happy, with some candy in hand for me.

He is a man like millions of others, pitted against the harshness of life, attached to his traditions and beliefs, proud of the Punjab, 'the richest state in India!' He isn't a Buddhist, but remains faithful to his Sikh roots. On the other hand, he respects the Dalai Lama, calling him 'a very good man'. He points out to me that the Tibetans exiled in India are richer than the Indians, and get more aid; but he says this without malice. That's just how it is; so much the better for them.

He shows me photos of his wife and children. He's a man with a ready smile, a very reliable driver. Like many men, he hates to ask for directions, which sometimes resulted in us getting lost. But it doesn't bother him, he just makes a half-turn and tries another road. On our way back to Delhi he stops at a truck stop, 'the best restaurant in north India,' he insists. The food is heavily spiced.

How could this man forget the violence he has lived through? Assuming that he even wanted to, how much time would it take him to accept nonviolence, to be touched by Buddhism? In his life, gripped by necessity as it is, where could he find the time to meditate, to listen, to read?

I wonder about that in the car, as I look at his hands grasping the heavy steering wheel, and his light blue turban carefully wrapped all around his head.

7

The Big Bang and Reincarnation

Are you the last Dalai Lama?

That's quite possible.

Why?

There are two sorts of reasons. First of all, political. For thirty-five years the Chinese have been repeating that I have only one desire: to restore the old kingdom as it used to be, to get back my servants, my privileges, and the thousand rooms of Potala.

What's your answer to that?

That the institution of the Dalai Lama is not under my jurisdiction. It's the business of the Tibetans themselves. I've said this clearly many times. If one day Tibet recovers its independence or at all events its autonomy – and I hope with all my heart that it will – that can only happen in a democratic manner. Will the Tibetans want to perpetuate the institution of the Dalai Lama? It's for them to decide. If a majority of them vote against it, I will retire immediately. In that case, I would in fact be the last Dalai Lama.

You said somewhere that under those conditions you would like to end your days in a monastery.

That idea doesn't displease me.

And the other reasons?

They're historical. Many people think the Dalai Lama is inseparable from the Tibetan people. That's false. Up until the sixteenth century Tibet got along fine without a Dalai Lama. It could be the same way tomorrow. I repeat: the next government of Tibet must be elected democratically. That's indispensable.

Could another Dalai Lama be born outside Tibet?

Why not? One was a native of Mongolia.

What are your relations with Mongolia today?

Very lively, and they go back very far. Mongolia is a country deeply marked by Buddhism. I visited it in 1979 when it was still Communist, like all the republics of the USSR. The people's attitude toward me seemed as spontaneous and warm as that of the Tibetans. I felt they were very close to me, and that greatly moved me. I will return there soon.

Is Buddhism still alive there?

Yes, it seems that way to me. We keep up very close ties on that score. Mongolian students, from different parts of the country, come here to India, to our various centers. And in turn some of us go to Mongolia.

And your relations with Nepal? Bhutan?

As long as it's just a question of people, our relations are excellent. On the governmental level, it's different. Since Tibet was annexed, these countries have common frontier with China. And that changes everything.

Needless to say, the idea that women were born to make men unhappy is widespread throughout the world and throughout history. Despite his enormous lucidity, the Buddha unfortunately didn't always escape this rule. He described women as mostly 'mad and wicked', fierce 'like brigands' and, of course, liars by nature. He long exhorted his first disciples, those at least who wanted to become monks, to do without women. For months the Buddha even refused to open his door to his father's second wife, who had raised him with loving care. Clothed in rags, she pleaded each day for a word or a glance. He didn't answer her.

Years passed before he allowed the foundation of women's communities. As for whether a woman could reach illumination as a man could, Sakyamuni consented to admit this only after long debates with his disciples, but regretted it shortly afterwards.

There is no doubt that from the standpoint of the spiritual life women were considered inferior.

This exclusion is curiously universal. In the sixteenth century, a council sharply divided the Catholic Church on the matter of the quality of woman's soul (though its existence was approved). Even today the ordination of women priests by the Anglican Church brought shocked objection from some pious souls. Pope John Paul II has just emphatically reaffirmed that in the Catholic Church only men can be priests.

For a long time, especially in southern Asia, women have had to observe precise rules in their dealings with begging monks. In filling up the alms bowl they couldn't touch the food. They couldn't walk on the plaited mat where a monk was sitting. They could never be the first to speak, never take off their clothes in front of him, or sit in any posture that might arouse desire.

In some cases, monks were even forbidden to ride on mares or she-asses. In the presence of a woman the bonzes of Cambodia hid their faces behind a fan (so as not to see or not to be seen?).

These prohibitions were rather quickly slackened in China, Japan, and still more in Tibet (no doubt under the influence of Tantrism). We can see this in a story told in Paul Reps's *Zen Flesh, Zen Bones* of two Zen monks on a journey. As they come to a river in flood, a frightened woman approaches and asks them to help her cross the tumultuous waters. Her mother lives over on the other side, and she's seriously ill. Both of these monks have taken solemn vows never to touch the flesh of a woman, yet the first one takes hold of the woman without hesitation and helps her across. Once arrived on the other side, the woman thanks him and hastens off. The two continue on their way in silence.

After walking this way for half an hour, the second monk, who has been fuming the entire time, suddenly asks the first,

'How could you break your vows? How did you dare touch the body of the woman?'

The other one looks at him and says, 'I left the girl back there? Are you still carrying her?'

Today the rule of celibacy remains just as strict for the monks as for the nuns (*bhiksus* and *bhiksunis*). But you will still see monks strolling freely through the streets of McLeod Ganj, entering the stores, chatting with men and women passersby. It isn't rare to see a monk dining privately with a foreign woman, usually one of his disciples.

Is it still a sign of negative karma *to be reborn in the body of a woman?*

In the past, women were undoubtedly looked down upon. Like other countries, Tibet established a clear-cut male predominance. Then little by little things changed. Today, if we compare ourselves with India or China, the condition of women in Tibet is certainly better. But things remain to be done.

In Buddhism, and especially in the Mahayana tradition, the two sexes are theoretically equal. After ordination *bhiksus* and *bhiksunis* have in principle the same rights and duties. It is said that Buddhism was vigorously propagated in Tibet by the two wives (one Nepalese, the other Chinese) of the King S'rong T'san Gampo. Upon their death, something extraordinary happened: Avalokiteshvara, the *bodhisattva* of compassion, had just decided to save the world from suffering, from the cycle of *samsara*. He succeeded, by an extreme effort, while closing his eyes. But when he was obliged to open them, he saw that suffering was still there, that *samsara* had once again filled the world.

Then a tear of sadness and discouragement flowed down his cheek. That tear splashed on the two queens, thus revealing their destiny as protectresses and consolers. They are called 'Green Tara' and 'White Tara'. They are often fused into a single deity called 'Tara', who is venerated in all the aspects of daily life. She is called 'the mother of all the Buddhas'. She soothes and she reassures. Some very beautiful texts of poetry are dedicated to her.

The Buddhist pantheon is too complex for us to review in detail, and it varies from school to school. In it we see different superimposed hierarchies of buddhas, which divide and subdivide several times. This edifice is dominated by five entities, known as 'the victorious ones' (*Jinas*) or the buddhas of meditation. They correspond to the five sense organs, the five colours, and the five virtues. They rule time and space. Each one has his own special invocation and his own peculiar attributes. Each one also has a sort of 'son', a spiritual reflection who is, properly speaking, a *bodhisattva*. Thus Avalokiteshvara, 'he who looks down', that is, the compassionate one [of whom the line of the Dalai Lama is the incarnation] has been engendered by the Jina Amitabha, 'the infinite light', the Lord of the West.

In this refined, singular construct, which our minds, trained in other concepts, have a hard time grasping, the feminine force called 'Arya Tara' holds one of the highest ranks.

She isn't there by chance. When she had attained the first degree of awakening, and could lay claim to a superior degree of existence, and she saw the numerical supremacy of the male powers, she cried out, 'I want to reach the Buddha-state, but in the form of a woman.' She wanted somehow to show that she could lay claim to the same level as Avalokiteshvara. And she succeeded.

And yet discrimination persists. It's hard to specify the reasons and the limits, but the *bhiksunis* aren't viewed with the same goodwill and the same respect as the *bhiksus*. Even though they theoretically observe the same rules.

Why?

I don't see it clearly, but I'm aware of this discrimination, and last year I called for a conference about it. It lasted four days. Teachers came from all over the world, from the West and from Japan. All together we discussed a large number of problems, specifically concerning the condition of women, sexual life, and other problems occurring periodically everywhere in the world. One *bhiksuni* spoke out on the inequality that weighs down on the nuns. Another, an elderly European woman, told her own story of difficulties quite simply. Her story touched me quite deeply, and I started to cry. Yes, without a doubt, the situation can be improved.

The feminist struggles of the '60s and '70s brought some results, at least in theory. But in fact we're still familiar with another form of discrimination: in such areas as women's salaries, their place in the political realm, control of the media, not to mention the troubles and traumas of everyday life, domestic abuse, rape, sexual harassment. After the hopes for liberation and equality in the previous decades, a sort of disillusionment seems to have come crashing down on a whole generation of women, now in their forties, some divorced, unemployed, consigned to loneliness in a society both timid and paralyzed by various stages of crisis.

I have heard echoes of these disappointed hopes. Here in Asia the conditions are obviously different. Something has to be done. And to begin with, in education.

We have to acknowledge that women have the same intellectual qualities as men. For an example we can cite an exceptional woman who lived in the fourteenth century, Samding Dorjee Phagmo. She was recognized as a woman lama and thus acquired the power to become reincarnated, according to our traditions. As a result, she was the beginning of a line of women lamas, who have succeeded one another to this day.

Are there other female lines?

Yes, four or five. At the outset we must reflect on what these successions of women lamas brought us, see what special and precious things their teaching has been able to offer us.

A marriage custom which has long existed among us is that the man would come and be installed in the family of the woman, and then the name of the family remained that of the woman.

Her name was passed down to the children?

Yes, the name of the mother. Of course, the Chinese invasion and exile have thrown these customs into confusion, but I find them wise. We have to recover this and other traditions and introduce into them the positive aspects we can find elsewhere.

In a state in southern India, Kerala, there is a matriarchal tradition. The women are often the owners and guardians of family property, which is passed on from woman to woman.

Yes, in Tibet, too, women could inherit.

Have those traditions changed with exile?

I don't think so. Of course, nowadays Chinese law has been imposed upon Tibet. But tradition becomes a way of resisting.

Here, as I said, we go to great lengths to maintain it, because it is our best weapon. For me there is no doubt that in the future the rights of women will be strictly guaranteed. We should even, on this occasion, get a new awareness of what it means to say, 'equality between men and women.'

If birth control is indispensable, which seems to be the case, women necessarily have to have a controlling hand in the process. They have to recover the right to give or refuse life.

I believe so too.

I imagine that the existence of 'masculinity' or 'femininity' must seem impossible from the standpoint of impermanence.

Like any existence that would claim to enjoy a stable quality. These notions have no meaning for us. They are simply attached to conditions, to circumstances (that is, to the cultural and historical environment), and these circumstances can change.

Could a woman be one of the next Dalai Lamas?

In theory there is nothing against it.

We rediscover her, as elsewhere (for example, in the area of science), the remarkable faculty of *adaptation* that Buddhism demonstrates today and that no doubt largely explains the many sympathies it awakens. The extreme flexibility and fluidity of its thought seems to be in tune with the movement of the world, that movement which it affirms and to which it submits. What remains striking is that this incessant adaptation, obviously accelerated by the century itself and all the shocks that have jolted it, has not changed the ancient foundations of Buddhism – impermanence, interdependence, compassion, and the necessary awakening. Sometimes it even reinforces them.

But now we have arrived at the subject of reincarnation. Here, I run into a solid obstacle, and I am quite open about it with my host. Since the beginning of our conversations, we have found a certain number of points in common. Here, however, is a point of divergence.

Buddhism has been built up and maintained on an idea of universality. What's good for one man is good for all men (and women). For more than a century we Westerners have gotten used to the ethnographic approach to behaviour and thinking (which includes religions). And to us reincarnation looks like a belief inherited from India and nowadays strictly limited to a single part of the world.

It's true that Pythagoras claimed to recall his earlier lives. In *The Republic*, Plato shows us dead warriors choosing the bodies for their next life. In keeping with his personality, Ajax chooses to be a lion, while the buffoon Thersites chooses to be an ape. Only the cunning Odysseus chooses the life of a peaceful man, who is left alone.

Still, it's hard to say that these beliefs, which seem reserved to a cultivated elite, are at the heart of Greek thought. In any case, as with the Hebrew Cabalists, they did not survive the fall of the ancient world and the triumph of Christianity in the West.

In India, these beliefs are still very much alive, adapted to Buddhism for its own purposes. Certain stages of the process of reincarnation, such as the voyage of the *bardo* after (what we call) death are often limited to Buddhist Tibet. The idea of universalism seems not to be at all present in this seeming regional folklore.

Reincarnation, in the Tibetan Buddhist sense, is not really part of any of our religions. That idea remains quite alien to us and is difficult to accept. It sometimes even prompts scorn and confusion.

Another difficulty relates to the scrupulous examination that Buddhism has always claimed as its method. Sakyamuni said it first: 'Observe this object that is now here.' We read in your Scriptures that nothing must be accepted unless it has been established, proved, and verified by experience. Well, far from being verifiable, reincarnation strikes us as precisely one of those 'beliefs' that in other domains Buddhism often invites us to reject. There seems to be a contradiction here.

There is a third difficulty, which is tied in with the very teaching of Buddhism. In our discussions we've said that it seemed altogether possible that on some points Buddhism agreed with the (provisional) conclusions of modern scientists. Both maintain that nothing is stable, neither in matter nor in the mind, that everything ceaselessly dissolves and is recomposed, and that in particular our 'self', so proudly unfurled in the West, is nothing but a puff of wind, an illusion, a fleeting reality, strictly unfindable. As a result, if nothing of our self subsists, what is this self, what is this ego that gets reincarnated? Something of us, some quality peculiar to us, must be able to subsist and transmit itself.

What does reincarnation mean to you today? Is it an allegory or a fact? And what strength do you draw from it?

Buddhists says that rebirth is a reality. It's a fact. In the cycle of rebirths, which we call *samsara*, from time to time there occurs the phenomenon of reincarnation.

First of all, let's make a distinction. The cycle of rebirths, *samsara*, is the very condition of all life. No existence escapes it, unless it gets to *nirvana*. This condition is painful, because it obliges us to live and live again, on levels that can be worse than those we have known.

If rebirth is an obligation, reincarnation is a choice. It is the power, granted to certain worthy individuals, to control their future birth.

As was the case with the Buddha?

Exactly. And with many others. When it reaches a certain degree of quality, which we have called 'subtle consciousness', our mind cannot die, in the ordinary sense of the word. It is given the power to become reincarnate in another body. This is especially the case for the *bodhisattvas*, as we said. At the very gates of *nirvana*, they prefer to renounce it in order to remain in *samsara*, and continue to help us.

But how does one know that this or that individual is the reincarnation of this or that other?

That *is* a crucial point. To begin with, we meet people who have detailed recollections of their earlier lives.*

---

* At Dharamsala, and in other Buddhist centers, this certitude is widely shared. An individual who bears unquestionable signs of reincarnation is called a *tulku*. And there are many of them. In a souvenir shop, run by an Indian, I met a German photographer who is doing a book on the *tulkus*. He has already photographed several dozen of them, and he showed me the questionnaire he asks them to fill out. They have to indicate their last name, first name, date of birth, address, and the Buddhist school to which they belong. On the last line is: 'Reincarnation of . . .?'

Or who claim to remember them. What's interesting is that they've never been a toad or a wretched slave. In general, they have lived in the desirable body of a famous hetaera or that of an Egyptian high priest.

Of course. There are liars everywhere.

*And, on the other hand, the texts indicate that there are six possible conditions for a person after death, which are called the paths of transmigration.**

Right.

Of these six conditions, the hardest to obtain is precisely the human condition. The only hope to reach the Buddha-state is to be reborn as a human being, but that's also a rare case. By comparison, an ancient legend tells us to imagine a tortoise living at the bottom of the ocean, from whence its head emerges every hundred years, and a ring floating on the troubled surface of the waters: there is as much chance of the head of the tortoise passing through the ring as there is of a human becoming reincarnate in another human. How, then, can you explain that all those who recall their past lives always talk about advantageous human situations, and that the tulkus are proliferating around us?

Reincarnation in a human is difficult, but much less than the Indian legend says it is. The phenomenon exists, we are certain of it. Right here at Dharamsala, we know several persons who

---

* Those conditions are those of a god, of a human being, an *asura* (roughly translated as 'demon'), an animal, a *preta* (starving, thirsty being), and finally of an infernal creature that wanders from frozen hells to scorching hells, from the hell of bronze to the hell of the dung heap to the hell of thorns.

have very clear memories of their previous existence, and whose conditions of life back then had nothing extraordinary about them. In particular, we have known Indian children, two little girls aged three and four, who recounted in detail episodes from earlier lives. Their parents couldn't believe it, but when we took them to where they seemed to have lived, they recognized the places.

Such examples of recognition are cited rather frequently. The Dalai Lama himself, at the age of three, recognized certain objects as having belonged to his predecessor, who had died several years before. When he caught sight of these objects, he grabbed hold of them saying, 'They're mine, they're mine!' and everyone was convinced that he really was the reincarnation they were looking for. Other signs had led those conducting the inquiry to the house of his parents. When he was officially recognized, he was taken away from his family and brought to a monastery. His training as the Dalai Lama began. That happened in1938.

Some hasty journalists still present the Dalai Lama as a living god. For a Buddhist this expression makes no sense. The institution of the Dalai Lama, a temporal and spiritual authority, is actually subject to two requirements: he must be the guaranteed reincarnation of the one who has preceded him, and hence of all the others, going back to the fourteenth century. The Tibetans are deeply attached to this notion of lineage, of a very high spiritual energy that is transmitted from individual to individual and that, each time, can be intensified. The present Dalai Lama claims to have had long discussions, in dreams, with his predecessor, and to have taken his advice.

On the other hand, by his very function the Dalai Lama is considered to be a 'manifestation' or 'emanation' of

Avalokiteshvara himself, the white lotus, the great *bodhisattva* of compassion. Thus he would be the seventy-fourth descendant of another line, going back to a Brahman child who lived at the same time as the Buddha. Today Buddhists no longer seem to accept the idea that there really exists in heaven a 'being', a 'person' who becomes incarnate in human form. Rather they see that emanation as a particular force allowing the Dalai Lama to concentrate in his person the powers of compassion that each one of us possesses.

When asked if he is sure, now, that he really belongs to these two lineages, the Dalai Lama admits he is slightly at a loss. The answer, he says, isn't simple. But he admits that, relying on his education and his practice of Buddhism, he feels 'spiritually connected' to the thirteen previous Dalai Lamas, to Avalokiteshvara and the Buddha Sakyamuni himself.

You can also consider reincarnation from another point of view, by reflecting on the evolution of our planet, and even of our universe. Today we are here, we see the world around us, we know that it stretches to unimaginable distances. But we also know, or at any rate the science tells us, that this world hasn't always been here.

For a long time people believed that it was. The universe was supposed to be infinite, eternal. One of the great discoveries of astrophysics in the twentieth century was to give the universe an age and a history.

You're referring to what is called the big Bang. But how, and why did the Big Bang happen? Nobody can say. Well,Buddhim has one constant: every event has to have a cause. As far as the universe extends in space, it is subject to impermanence and *samsara*. As far back as it goes in time, whatever happens has to have a cause.

Assuming the Big Bang was an event. At any given moment all that we see is an extremely dense state of what was destined to become the matter that makes up the stars – and us. But we can't speak of an 'explosion', as the term Big Bang suggests.

And beyond that state of matter?

We don't see anything. That's what astrophysics has found. The Big Bang is the first point of our possible reading of the universe, the beginning of our discourse about it. It's not necessarily the actual beginning. What existed before the Big Bang (assuming that there was something) is a subject we can't talk about. We can only speculate. But how can you imagine what was here before there was anything?

In any case, the Buddhists say that the age we live in is the result of the ages that preceded it, and so on all the way back to the origin of time.
So why the Big Bang? What caused it?

The Christians have an answer.

I'm familiar with it. For my part, there are two answers that I can't accept. The first consists in saying there is no cause. Things just happened like that, all by themselves. From our point of view, this is unacceptable. The second answer is the divine solution that one fine day God decided to create the world. We don't accept that either.

Why not?

Because that answer raises too many questions. Why did the creator create? Who created the creator? Did he create himself? Did this creator have a beginning? Will he have an end? Is creation a permanent process? And so on.

If the creator himself is permanent, creation is permanent.

Which leads us to other questions, such as, it the creator a being with total compassion? Is he omnipotent? Is he omniscient?

Why, if he is all-powerful, did he create a world so obviously imperfect? Why did he create this world rather than another? Why did he take so much time to create it?

Actually, from our standpoint the theory of the creator poses a lot more problems than it solves.

Then what is the Buddhist explanation?

The question of the origin of the world is not posed in these terms in the ancient texts. The Buddhist universe is made up of an infinity of worlds, something like disks slipped over the axis of the mythical Mount Meru. Around that axis are located seven mountain ranges, as many oceans, and four large continents at the four cardinal points. Each universe has nine planets, twenty-seven or twenty-eight 'celestial reference points', and many stars.

This cyclical and repetitive aspect of space recurs in the ancient conception of time that originates in Brahmanism. The temporal cycles, the *yugas* and *kalpas*, recur eternally. They are divided into a certain number of periods of unequal duration, which can exceed a million years, some of which are called 'incalculable'. Some of these periods are times of destruction, others of recomposition, and others of stability.

In the course of the periods of recomposition (also known as 'empty periods'), the particles of space subsist. They will serve to recompose matter. The whole of these temporal movements is contained in a 'great cycle,' a *mahakalpa*, which transcend knowledge and any measurement

These long speculative descriptions – elaborated by successive schools and often contradicting one another – run counter to Sakyamuni's fundamental recommendation not to plunge 'the cord of thought into the impenetrable'. The question of the eternity of the universe, and consequently of its origins, actually seems to have been part of the 'fourteen unexplained views'. The Buddha even said, 'Knowledge of all these things cannot make anyone take one step forward on the road to holiness and peace.' His only answer was silence.

Nevertheless, as the Dalai Lama told me on several occasion, on the one hand, events without a cause cannot be accepted, and on the other hand, it is absolutely necessary to pay attention to the advances of science to modify, if need by, the Scriptures. Thus there is no reason to be surprised at how little he insists on going back to ancient theories. He prefers to stick to the Big Bang and to try to find in it an explanation that jibes with the essentials of Buddhist teaching.

Apropos of the Big Bang, I remind him that this ironic expression, coined by astrophysicist Fred Hoyle, who was opposed to it, is based on an idea formulated by a Belgian priest, Fr. Geogres-Henri Lemaitre. Even in scientific theories often enough it's possible to find a trace of 'hidden metaphysics'. The idea of an 'explosion', of a brutal, luminous beginning of the world, can in fact be harmonized with the biblical account of Creation.

Certain beings must have rejoiced, at a given moment, over the existence of the universe. And that's why this universe is there.

Who are these beings, or who were they?

Not human beings.

Extraterrestrials?

No, not in the sense you give that word. These are beings who enjoy a mind and feeling. When we speak of 'mind', we know that there are different categories, different levels of mind. Some of these levels are coarse. The mind is then directly bound up with a body, and it ceases to exist with it. In that case, when the functions of the body stop, the functions of mind do the same.

But we have seen that the mind can also raise itself.

Up to the highest levels, up to the 'subtle mind' or 'subtle consciousness'. Conceptual thought has its limits, as we all know. That is why on the difficult road to knowledge most traditions have tried to take what might be called ' a direct route'. Mysticism, yoga, certain forms of meditation and ecstasy mark that direct way, which culminated in awakening.

That's the state where we are granted a flawless knowledge of all things?

Yes, down to the last detail. According to Tibetan tradition, this direct approach – which can lead us by experience all the way to the origins of the world – is extremely difficult. It presupposes that our mind has been developed and refined down to its highest quality of subtlety, which tears it away from the temporal cycles. Some of my friends who are still alive have known such moments.

Then the person remembers a past life?

Not one life, but hundreds, thousands of lives. The mind can't be born from anything except mind. Consequently, the subtle mind can't have a beginning. When subtle consciousness appears in all its clarity, the questions aren't raise din the same way, the very idea of a beginning disappears.

❖

The great Japanese Zen master, Dogen Zenji, tells the following story on this topic:

A highly respected Zen master was fanning himself.

A monk approached and asked him, 'The nature of the wind is permanent, and there is no place that it does not reach. So why must you still fan yourself?'

'Even if you understand that the nature of the wind is permanent,' the master replied, 'you didn't understand the significance of its presence everywhere.'

'What, then, is the significance of its presence everywhere?' the monk asked.

The master was content to go on fanning himself.

The monk bowed in deep respect.

In other words, Dogen Zenji explains that those who say that one shouldn't use a fan because the wind is permanent, and that one should know the existence of the wind without using a fan, know neither permanence nor the nature of the wind.

Mystery, depth, and limit of knowledge: awakening gives it all, though it can't really be communicated, except by a gesture such as fanning. The Buddhist masters recommend that one not practice Buddhism in the hope of receiving knowledge as a reward. That would be the wrong approach. Awakening is not necessarily given to those who believe they deserve it. Some reach it and some don't. In any case, as Dogen Zenji says, 'The limits of the knowable are unknowable.'

All these references spin uselessly in my head while I try to 'understand' – knowing that it's impossible – what the Dalai Lama is saying as he speaks to me all at once about subtle mind, reincarnation, and the origin of the world. There is a link between these three notions, but it remains rather obscure to me.

The Dalai Lama was once asked, What is it that is reborn? His answer is the 'I'. His questioner, quite properly surprised, replied that he doesn't know what that 'I' is. 'If I am reborn,' he says, 'I don't know that it's I. I no longer remember what I was before. Who am I?'

In this answer the Dalai Lama points out that even in this life, we can remember certain experiences and forget others, all the more so when it's a matter of other existences.

Nothing permits me to maintain that we will be able to remember one day what we have experienced, our acts, our emotions, the objects that surrounded us. The fact that we remember nothing in no way justifies the conclusion that, 'That wasn't me', that I am now a new creature, unique in the history of the world.

Why do the immense majority of men and women remember nothing?

Because at the moment of death the level of consciousness – the intermediary state between one life and another – becomes more subtle. It's at this subtle level that the memories of preceding life catch hold, in order to pass into another life. But out of weakness, out of lack of training and concentration, the great majority of individuals remain on the level of the conscious mind that we call 'coarse'.

So those who have some experience of more profound consciousness have a better chance to remember their past lives?

Yes, undoubtedly.

If I understand you correctly, this subtle consciousness exists independently of the body and the brain?

Yes. It is bound up with the appearance of consciousness in the human being, and it is always present. It subsists even when other levels of consciousness are obliterated.

Then it's indestructible?

In a way. And that's the reason why it's reincarnated. To get back to the Big Bang, or to the origin of the world, one can even think that the subtle mind, with its incomparable force, is the first creative principle.

I imagine that the Buddha Sakyamuni penetrated this subtle mind?

He was a manifestation of it, even though he was born a prince, lived as a beggar, and was seen by thousands of persons. His life, manifested in this way, was a little bit like a role. He played that role for a human lifetime, to come to our aid. But his subtle mind, even before his birth, had already eliminated all the obstacles to perfect vision.

Another manifestation of subtle mind is the preservation of the body after clinical death. Thus the body of my tutor remained intact for thirteen days before beginning to decompose. Another lama, an exceptional man, was able to preserve his body uncorrupted for seventeen years.

How do you explain that?

By the high quality of subtle mind, which is always there, and whose force is such that it maintains the integrity of the body. Sometimes one even sees on the face of the dead person – this was the case with my tutor – more luminousness, more serenity. On the last day of this kind of survival, a little bit of liquid appears, and then decomposition begins. This liquid is the sign of the departure of the subtle mind.

And the search for another body?

Yes.

Then it's the subtle mind that is reincarnated?

Yes, but this mind, it has to be repeated, is not what we call *atman*. It's not the soul, as you say, which is eternal by its essence. We don't recognize any particular essence, any stable and independent entity attached to the individual. Our consciousness is perennially changing. Nothing is permanent, nothing can be transmitted without profound modifications.

You have said that death, a normal and inevitable process, is for you like changing old and worn-out clothes, rather than a real end.

Exactly. And if we want to die well, we must learn to live well. The experience of death is extremely important for us, because our state of mind at that moment can decide the quality of our future rebirth. We can even, at the moment of dying, make a special effort. In the course of it meditation can reach an unequaled summit, as shown by the preservation of the body. By the way, the hope of every true Buddhist is to die before one's master, to be soothed and guided by him at the last moment.

It is customary, among those who believe in another life or in other forms of life, to criticize sharply the materialistic attitude, which is so prevalent in the West. Materialists believe, following the lead of all the appearances, that death is the end of life, in any case of a life, of our life. This attitude, superbly described by Montaigne in his Essays, supposedly leads to brutal, egotistical behaviour that has no concern for tomorrow or for the future of the earth.

This criticism, which sometimes flows from the pens of Buddhist writers, has always struck me as superficial. First of all, nothing allows us to say that those who believe in this life alone don't care at all about the earth that they will leave to their children. Apart from that, it is permissible to find within the very limits of human life, which goes from nothingness to nothingness, the prime reason for its dignity and beauty.

In Buddhist tradition, which is claimed to be based on experience and the recognition of facts, the threat of rebirth in lower bodies, even those of animals or demons, serves quite like the policeman's billy club, prompting us to behave better in the life that has been given to us here and now. We know what difficulties confront the establishing of a civil morality, the lay morality for which the Dalai Lama often appeals. Perhaps we still need, at least for those of us who can't accept the idea (though it's quite simple) of a total and definitive death (save for our elementary particles, which will recombine), that fear of punishment in some hell, or the hope of an eternal reward.

Since it seems its end is predictable, I prefer not to get into this discussion. It seems a little more interesting to continue on the Buddhist path, where life and death are conceived as a whole. Death – and more precisely the passage, or *bardo*, that heads from one life to another – is often perceived as a mirror where life is reflected in its entirety. Thus death is learned during life. Living well is learning to die well, so as to live again better. The holy Tibetan poet Milarepa put it this way: 'This thing called a corpse, which so frightens us, lives with us, here and now.'

❖

We are afraid to die because we don't know the day nor the hour, because death can surprise us at any moment. Because we fear what comes after death, we are afraid of finding ourselves in an unknown and disagreeable place, filled with anxiety.

Even Buddhists feel this way?

Certainly. Don't forget that the obligation to be reborn isn't considered a reward. On the contrary. I'm trying to tell you that reincarnation, which is a choice, is profoundly connected to a certain level of the life of the mind. If that level is reached, the subtle mind that we have developed – can choose its next destination. Thus it is a step toward liberation, a possible amelioration. Without that choice, rebirth is a slipping back into *samsara*.

Can reincarnation occur somewhere other than on earth?

Certainly. On another planet, or even in another galaxy. The noble states of the mind can stretch out to infinity. That's one of our fundamental teachings.

And the mind can transform itself?

It can and it must. It can get rid of the impurities that contaminate it, and rise to the highest level. We all start off with the same capacities, but some people develop them, and others don't. we very easily get used to the mind's laziness, all the more easily because that laziness hides beneath the appearance of activity: we run right and left, we make calculations and phone calls. But these activities engage only the most elementary and coarse levels of the mind. They hide the essential from us.

Why is the mind tied to the body?

Because everything that changes must have substance, when we speak of the mind, we know well that it can't be seen or measured. It needs our substantial form, which comes to us from our parents, in keeping with the laws of heredity. This substance is governed by the chromosomes, I believe. The mind represents the subtle and ungraspable energy that takes the body as its substance. At its highest level, as I said, this mind cannot disappear. Then it's considered a form of wisdom, it's the inner master, the supreme guru. It has transcended space and time.

And if one day science proves that reincarnation doesn't exist?

If it really does prove it, we'll have to give it up. And we will. But for the moment, to our eyes, rebirth and reincarnation are real, just as atoms are real. If some people don't believe that rebirth is a reality, we describe their attitude as ignorance.

So it's not a belief?

No. it's a physical phenomenon. According to our Scriptures, subtle particles existed in space before the Big Bang. They are still there. Did these spiritual particles, which constitute beings, give birth to the Big Bang? Why? How? We can't answer that.

The universe is eternal?

A particular universe can exist and disappear. Immense cycles can succeed one another. But the universe, as a whole, the universe-mind, is always there.

The nature of the Buddha exists in all things. But we can't know everything. Thus we don't know if even flowers can experience pleasure or pain.

In my childhood I saw my grandfather, a little peasant from the south of France, plant two similar tomato seedlings in a corner of his garden, in the same soil. Every day he gave it a thousand compliments. Meanwhile, he never said a word or paid any attention to the second one.

Each year he showed us how the first plant bore more numerous and beautiful tomatoes than the second one. Was my grandfather playing a trick? Did he want to pass for a kind-hearted wizard? I never found out.

You'd have to go farther. You'd have to know, for example, if those reactions came from the plant itself or from some invisible beings.

We believe that subtle consciousness exists, and that it's the source of everything that we call 'creation'. In each individual, this subtle consciousness dwells from the beginning of time until access to the Buddha-state. That's what we call 'being'. This being can take on different forms, animal beings, human beings, and eventually Buddhas. This is the very foundation of the theory of rebirths. The subtle mind, over the long succession of centuries, from form to form, necessarily searches for the Buddha-state. When it reaches a high degree of quality in an individual, it chooses its next form. That is reincarnation.

Even if our religious or philosophical traditions often prevent us from going along with this idea, even if it remains alien to us, even if we lack direct experience of reincarnation, one can't help admiring the true grandeur of this vision. I return for an instant to the Surrealist manifesto of 1925, to that 'freedom of the mind in the mind', the supreme hope. Buddhism goes as far as possible in its quest for the highest form of the mystery that is the mind. To borrow the title of the poem, all of Buddhism is an 'inscription on the faith in mind'. By refusing to suppress the mind, it has gone even beyond the world.

Another way of speaking about that state of supreme consciousness, the goal of all practitioners of Buddhism, is the expression, highly mysterious in some ways and remarkably distant from us, of *tathagata*. The word means 'one who arrived somewhere' or 'from somewhere', and is applied to a number of great personages, one of whom is Sakyamuni.

We can try to approach it via the word *tathata*, which means 'the fact of being such'. The word is sometimes translated as 'suchness'. Once again words are a brake and a mask.

This 'fact of being such' is a higher kind of simplification. The mind attains such a lofty quality that it forgets itself. Nothing separated the particular being from itself or from other things. It is this way, it is that. It is assimilated to the rest of the world, without reflection, with doubt or distance. This assimilation is natural. The person who is the beneficiary of it might not even notice it.

As many Zen koans say, in order to attain the supreme truth it is enough to prepare tea correctly or wave a fan when it is hot. In one story, travellers meet an old man making his way through the mighty waters of a torrent with amazing agility. He leaps from rock to rock and slides into the torrents and eddies where no twenty-year-old athlete would venture. When asked his secret, he can't understand the question: he has lived next to the torrent since childhood and pays no attention to it. He has become the slippery rock, the churned-up water. He can no longer tell the difference between it and him.

In looking back at my notes from our conversations, I see that we talked very little about the gods. This is a little out of proportion with Tibetan Buddhism, since it has recognized and multiplied the divine forms, producing even more than Brahmanism. A fundamental distinction is made between the 'worldly' gods (i.e., those attached to the forms of the world, such as the sun, the moon, or a fountain) and 'the extra-worldly gods', who are detached from perceptible forms. These two categories are further divided and subdivided. All these divinities, whose leading characteristics are often inherited from Brahmanism, are not necessarily benevolent. Some can be fearful, like the frightening Marici, who is shown with the head of a lioness and who is the wife of the king of hell. By contrast, another goddess, Lhamo, who has the attributes of the very bloody Indian goddess Durga, is compassionate and reassuring. She sides with us against the demons who, like the gods, are many and hard to tell apart.

All these images of divinities, this great mist of gods, can serve as a support for prayer and meditation. As the mind gradually rises in its perception of itself, looking within rather than going astray outside, it perceives this infinity of forces and forms. To borrow an expression from Maurice Percheron, it is like 'the fires of a single diamond'. Bit by bit unity reveals itself, the unity that is inconceivable and that yet can be attained in the high subtlety of the mind.

It seems that contemporary Buddhism is adapting flexibly to the almost indiscernible movement of time. At its most refined level it is slowly abandoning the ancient notions and forms, like a traveller getting rid of extra baggage. Thus Buddhists are saying good-bye, but without haste, without denial, without revolution, to the mythological adventures of the gods and goddesses, to useless and even obscure beliefs, to everything that could pass for supernatural, that is to say for external.

In place of all that, mind is imposing itself, a creative mind capable of reaching great heights and familiar with eternity. According to the most refined (and difficult) teachings of Tantrism, that mind, freed from all excess baggage, sees the whole truth in this world and in the perception that we have of it. It is pointless to search, as is done in traditional Mahayana, beyond this mind in a forest of invisible beings. It's all here. Our effort must aim to seek out the purity of appearances, to see the phenomena – which contain all the truth – as laid bare, revealing their true nature.

The mind here becomes its own machine, its light, and its mirror. The divinities that one can invoke have lost all detached existence, they are now nothing but expressions of the true nature of what is. They can also be considered – and this is not a contradiction – as extensions of our thought.

Thus, as one Tibetan master, Chogyam Trungpa, writes, this work of the mind is 'one of the most advanced, the keenest, and most extraordinary perceptions ever developed. It is unusual and original. It is powerful, magical, and outrageous. But it is also extremely simple.'

The one question remaining – and the masters of Buddhist thought have not failed to ask it – is whether the mind itself might not be an illusion, the supreme illusion. We have already mentioned the mind's putting itself into a dizzy spin. The fact that it names and analyzes itself in no way proves its existence (contrary to Descartes' 'I think, therefore I am'). It could well be only one of the attributes of the great net of Maya, perhaps even the entire net, the illusion that envelopes us all, along with the gods and perhaps even the buddhas.

But that is another subject altogether. While acknowledging it, Buddhism generally does not take it up. Hesitating between a game of nothingness (where the mind, by its very nimbleness, ends by losing all its underpinnings and doubting its own existence) and the necessity of an everyday morality in this relative and suffering life, Buddhism always comes back to that practical and even pragmatic aspect. It shows us how to live. And it supposes a hidden world, where light and the void began, and will end, by fusing into one.

8

And Finally, The Void

The fundamental Scriptures of Mahayana comprise about a hundred volumes. A part of this canon bears the name of *Prajnaparmita*.

Prajna is a quality we all have, though it generally lies dormant in us. It is most often translated as 'wisdom,' but that is not exactly right. It is more of a predisposition to wisdom and awakening, which we can either awaken or allow to continue sleeping. *Prajnaparmita* is the achieving of *prajna* – it is a crossing over, the arrival at the end of the road.

A phrase attributed to the Buddha himself and called 'the great deliverance', 'the matchless mantra', says, 'Where there is form there is the void; and where there is the void, there is form.'

Can I hope to understand that mantra some day?

The void, *Sunyata*, among the four fundamental Buddhist notions (the three others being impermanence, interdependence, and suffering) is certainly the most mysterious and hard to grasp. What *is* this immense edifice of experience and thought that in the end only opens up on an absence of substance? What would be the foundation of that edifice and of the mind that built it? If the void is the only reality that isn't illusory, who escapes the net of *Maya*? Who has cast this net? Can one live over a dizzying void? Can we imagine a dream without a dreamer?

The void is a scientific notion. You said so yourself. We are empty, the matter that composes us is, so to speak, empty.

But I suppose that for Nāgarjunā the Buddhist conception of the void didn't have a scientific point of departure?

And why not? There are many paths leading to knowledge. And sometimes they cross.

Can one talk about the void without talking in the void?

I think so. First of all we have to make it clear that 'void' doesn't mean 'nothingness'. Certain commentators have wrongly accused Buddhists of 'nihilism'. The world we are a part of is not a being in itself, nor an ensemble of beings. It's a flux, a current of beings. That doesn't mean that it's nothing.

To say 'I am not' isn't the same thing as 'I am nothing'.

In no way. And that is explained this way: all things depend on other things. Nothing exists separately. I believe, by the way, that on this point contemporary science is moving along the same road as we are. We say this: on account of the influences they receive, things appear, exist, and disappear. Unceasingly. But they never exist by themselves.

Look at my hand, for example. It gives the impression of solidity, of coherence. It offers a precise form to those looking at it. It has all the appearances of an entity. But if I ask myself seriously, if I wonder, what is my hand? Is it this finger? Is it this part of the finger? No, I can only answer, my finger is my finger, it's not my hand. But in turn in it just an ensemble of fingers? No, since I can break those down into digits, and study, look at, name these digit, one at a time.

Why stop there anyway?

Of course! I can go down deeper and deeper into the matter that's here without ever really encountering my hand.

Yet you use your hand.

That's what it's there for. And I'm very satisfied with it. This combination of different elements, each one of which breaks down and all of which fit together is what we call 'a hand'. It's very simple. We designate it that way by a simple labour of the mind. That's what we call 'relative reality'.

Which depends on other elements than itself?

Exactly. Because nothing exists without a cause. The profound nature of this hand is to belong to a whole network of influences, none of which is lasting.

That's why this hand will one day cease to be your hand.

It won't have been that except for a very brief moment, if you compare it with the age of the world. A fleeting, almost imperceptible moment. We are all persuaded that we live independently one from another, that a hand, a sheet of paper have separate existences.

Our mind needs to separate and name things. It can't be content with a complex and confused vision of the world.

A complex vision that we must nevertheless admit and try to attain. Otherwise we are choosing to remain in illusion. If each living creature, if every object enjoyed an independent existence, no other factor could influence it. The relations you speak of would not exist. Now, we see that these influences, these relations, are multiple and incessant.

So that absence of independent existence is what you call 'empty'?

Precisely. Hence form is 'empty', that is to say, nonseparate, nonindependent. This form depends on a multitude of other factors. It is relative reality.

And why is the void form?

Because all form develops in that void, in that absence of independent existence. The void is there only to lead to form. It can't be otherwise. The void without form wouldn't make any sense. Thus we have a sheet of paper which is empty. Empty, that is full. Full of the entire cosmos.

In the Tantric tradition of the Vajrayana, the 'diamond vehicle', we see the disappearance even of the distinction between absolute reality and relative reality, between the 'not-born' and the 'born', or, if you will, between essence and existence. The definitive and unsurpassable truth can be given us in the world of senses by the technique known as 'sacred visualization'. It rejoins the *tathata*, the way things are. The phenomena cease to appear as phenomena. Actually a differentiation between ignorance and knowledge is no longer made; nothing remains to be searched for 'beyond'.

Unity imposes itself. It is dazzling. Now nothing separates the void and the light.

We have come – almost inevitably – to the delicate subject of 'virtuality', which for ten years or so has been gradually slipping into and even installing itself in the language of science, at the same time that it invades the new image factories.

Refusing to admit the creation of a world out of nothing, *ex nihilo*, because in that case the physicist would have strictly nothing to say in the face of the absence of matter, some of the boldest contemporary scientists, such as Michel Cassé, speak of a 'courage in the face of zero', and quite simply reject nothingness. They sharply distinguish between the metaphysical void, or nothingness, a pure concept of the mind, and the quantum void, which they see as populated by an infinity of 'virtualities'.

This void is not nothing. It supposes the existence of a field, but that field escapes us. It isn't detectable. We can see its effects, because it links real particles to one another, and it even seems agitated to us, but we can't observe it. That's why we call it empty while it is full – full of the virtualities of matter.

To arrive at apparent existence, the conjunctions of virtual particles are only waiting to be activated, and the mere fact of observing them can play a determining role. Here we are very close to the absence of duality – between the observer and the observed – that has been repeatedly pointed out in the history of Hinduism and Buddhism. 'The thing that is seen is forever inseparable from the thing that sees,' said Kun Phyen Pema Karpo in the sixteenth century.

Michel Cassé goes so far as to say that 'knowledge *of the state of the void* has become a necessary condition for building a coherent model of nature.' He sees that void as 'something that is full and with a destiny' and places it 'at the cosmic and logical summit of discourse about origins.' He even writes toward the end of his book: 'To be in the void is to be home.'

No Buddhist teacher would find fault with that.

For the moment the physicists who venture into these territories are rather rare. Most prefer to stick to matter as it appears to us. And this matter seems in their eyes to keep its traditional meaning: something solid, heavy, full. The Big Bang seems to them the strict limit beyond which nothing can be said, thought, or imagined. It is true that it is hard to consider matter as void, as bit by bit practically dematerializing after centuries of observation.

Here is where the flexibility of Buddhism can help us to accept what we ourselves have discovered, and what the usual words prevent us from saying.

Still, the Dalai Lama points out to me that when we have designated things, we can say that they depend on our mind.

'Thus the Big Bang, like matter, perhaps depends upon our mind, and even on a need of our mind. So it forms part of relative reality. Today we call it the Big Bang. Tomorrow we'll no doubt give it another name. let's not allow ourselves to be imprisoned by words. This set and that set are ephemeral. Let's accept the void with a smile, and since everything depends on our mind, let's have confidence in our mind.'

He reminds me that this confidence, obviously, must not be blind. In this regard Buddhism has an immense arsenal of precautions to defend the mind against the mind and to bring it to its own summit. The supreme step leads to the disappearance of that mind, of the demons, of the Buddha himself. The void is the great goal. When the ultimate truth is attained, Milarepa sang:

> *If there is no meditator, no object to meditate on,*
> *If there are no signs of accomplishment,*
> *No stages nor road to travel,*
> *No ultimate wisdom, no body of Buddha,*
> *Nirvana too does not exist.*
> *All that is only words, ways of speaking.*

It's useless to pretend that we can begin with this ideally desired disappearance, this access to the plenitude of the void. If we were to proclaim that right from the start, it would only lead us to lonely discouragement, the fruit of nihilism, or to the chaotic violence of egoism: since nothing exists, since I am not controlled by any superior authority, why not abandon myself to my most demanding instincts?

The Dalai Lama concluded our conversations with this thought:

One thing can't be doubted, the 'possibility of a quality' is within us. It is called *prajna*. We can deny everything, except that we have the possibility of being better.

Simply reflect on that.

He seized both my hands and held them for a long time in his, and looked at me with a smile.

Like all conversations, this one leads us to silence.